THERE IS
NO LUCK
IN SUCCESS

J.L. TORRES

WRITERS REPUBLIC L.L.C.
515 Summit Ave. Unit R1
Union City, NJ 07087, USA

Website: *www.writersrepublic.com*
Hotline: *1-877-656-6838*
Email: *info@writersrepublic.com*

Ordering Information:
Quantity sales. Special discounts are available on quantity purchases by corporations, associations, and others. For details, contact the publisher at the address above.

Library of Congress Control Number:		2021915385
ISBN-13:	978-1-63728-734-7	[Paperback Edition]
	978-1-63728-735-4	[Hardback Edition]
	978-1-63728-736-1	[Digital Edition]

Rev. date: 08/04/2021

FOREWORD

This book was written so that people who though that inflation, and other world problems were out of hand are right, but you still can perform to your fullest. Just because inflation, insurance, Housing, Transportation, and other world problems are out of hand, does not mean that all other possibilities ha.ve ended. This book was written al.so to give you as at reader an idea in that you are your own person. "It matters not how straight the gate, how charged with punishments the scroll, I am the master of my fate: I am the captain of my soul." You can think about anything you want to. You can talk about anything you want to, and most important, You can do anything you want to.

Successfully Yours:
J. L. Torres
Author

CONTENTS

Section 1: There Is No Luck In Success 1

Preface 3
Articles to Newspapers.. 7
Author's Poems and Quotations 14
M.I.A 26
Ten Commandments To A Better Relationship............................. 28
Contemplating Future Possibilities 29
Days to Graduation 33
Shop Experience.. 40
Wedding Day 44
Potential Accomplishments For Future Ventures.......................48
Bitter Grape...........Sour Victory...54
Book 59
Future Homes 61

Section 2: There Is No Luck In Success 69

There Is No Luck in Success 71
Successful People and How They Became Successful.......................75
Dreams and Some Inspirational Quotations 79
Conquering What You Want Out Of Life....................................82
Recognizing Your Abilities 85
Learning From Mistakes... 88
Reading and Gathering Information..92
Analyzing Your Abilities...96
Doing or Making Something..99
What Are You Creating and Who Are You Creating For 103
Controlling Your Mind 107
The Last Thing To Do..111
4-I8-2I-7-I9 114
About the Author...119

SECTION 1

THERE IS NO LUCK
IN SUCCESS

Thus far I have written about things that a person must and mustn't do in order to succeed. Now I will focus on some personal experiences that actually happened or things that you can do to prevent them from happening, so that success *can* come about in a faster paste. You will see from reading this book that all a person really needs to succeed in life is a Desire. Yes, a desire to want something and going after it as if there would be no tomorrow. You should never take anything for granted, even if you think that something must have been done by now; Check it out, it may make you famous or rich or both. Personally I like to write about what I believe in or what I envision will happen or what might happen, just in case it does happen, I will then be able to prove what I said or thought or wrote back than (now). I will herein include writings that I have written about that I thought at the time were important. I have written four different articles and mailed to a News Paper (Hartford Courant), I don't know if any were ever put in the Editors Colum. The first one was what I thought about the space shuttle explosion (Challenger). The tragic truth that wasn't so. The accident that never was. The second article was about Prejudice in a Capitalist Society. The third article was to inform some readers about Puerto Rico and a very short history about the Island, from beginning to present. The fourth article was about Terrorism as I saw what it was doing what it may do if We (U.S Government) don't act now to put a stop to it, at least when it concerns our citizens or American interests. I will include all of our articles in full, plus some that I have not mailed to anyone but retained for this particular purpose (book material). I will also include some of my ideas and see where they will fall in history. I write all this because I really think that I was brought into this world for a purpose, I write it because I want the readers to know that I too started as you all did, and here I am now. I don't know what my future will be like but I want to start shaping it now, so it be a good one, whatever it will be. I believe that our destiny is really up to each one of us. I will talk about my birthplace and do research about what some call the Puerto Rico Problem. Well let's get right down to it. The first four pages are the articles I sent to the News Paper, and will continue from there on. May this part touch you as it did me and be as informative as the second part.

PREFACE

I would have to say that I always wanted to live the most beautiful life that anyone could ever live. For as long as I can remember I wanted to be a very rich man, and said to myself that I will never stop trying until this goal is accomplish. I would spend as much time as I possibly can on books, I mean I would spend hours reading; I read because I knew that the more I read about a specific subject the more I would know and understand it. I started reading in 1973 (I started to write down all the books I read) but really wasn't reading to gain knowledge but rather to say that I read books and give a list of which they were and impress those who I gave list to; After a while though I began to really get into what I was reading and once I started reading a book I really couldn't put it down until I was finished reading it from cover to cover. Then I started Reading for pleasure and for knowledge. On Tuesday May 29, 1979, I realized that what I was reading was influencing me and making me more intelligent (the more I read the smarter I became and soon people would sometimes ask what I was talking about, I would then have to rephrase what I had said, (in some cases it may me feel good). I realized in Senior day in High School that all those years in school wasn't doing me any good and I wanted better for myself. I also made a personal promise to myself that I would someday I write a book about myself and everything happening to me, even if it never got publish, I was going to try and not stop until I one way or another get it publish . I would really like to see my name in print, especially to something that other people would want to read and hopefully praised me for it. I think this would be a momentous feeling, one to 1ast for infinity and to cherish for life. I would try as hard as I could to share everything I knew with as many interested people as possible. I f I didn't know the answer to a question asked of me by someone interested I would find someone who would be able to answer the question fully and accurately. For those who needed special help in whatever field, I would (if I could afford it) provide professional counseling. I strongly believe that if trouble youths or anyone in particular having some sort of troubles understanding something, he/she should *have* the opportunity to talk with a social worker, free of charge. This could stop that individual from doing something foolish, I believe that if people could talk to train professionals about what is bothering then (at no cost to them) a lot of people would not be in the negative situation that they are now in. The insurance companies could provide this service, since they are the ones in charge *of* paying for ones ills, be it physical, or psychological. The Insurance Companies can prevent all sort of community problems by lending a helping hand at a time of need to an emotional person, in need of someone to sort out their (or help to sort out their) problems. Every person should have the privilege of seeking medical attention be physical or mental, even if that person doesn't actually need it, to a lot of people just knowing that this help is provided, if ever its needed is a relief in itself. People that are in prisons should be taught even by force if need be to read and write and possibly get an education for themselves in the process. They should learn how to better communicate with people in general and know the laws of the United States, so when they are let out of prison they can better understand how the laws apply to them and everyone else in general, what they can and what can rot do, and what will happen when and if they break the law. Those who want to learn can be treated better so those who don't want to learn will sooner or later become encourage to try and follow those who are making the change over and thus life becomes somewhat easier and better to deal with for everyone involved, and hopefully a repeat of a criminal acts will not occur. This book deals with the first twenty nine years of my life, in it I will talk about the things that I did and the things that I saw and basically what everyone was doing. I also want to point out that the way of life back then (1980) was (is) much different than it will be by the time this book becomes Publish. It really cannot be compare because the days past will become obsolete. (In my personal life, as well as chronologically). I would demonstrate how I made myself change, and what was going through my mine at the time. The most important reason that caused me to change was the idea that I had in mind about writing a book. I started to seriously think about it on May 29, 1979, even though I started a diary on October 4, 1977 with the hope that I would someday write a book or that someone would write one about me, but the possibility of that happening is very slim indeed, so I couldn't wait for someone to do that so I thought I can start now and finish later, this way things could hopefully move faster, especially since I have everything in a chronolic manner.

ARTICLES TO NEWSPAPERS

The Tragic Truth That Wasn't So
(The Accident That Never Was)

As discovered by this writer, the truth is revealed.

No life was lost in the explosion of challenger, on its twenty-fifth mission. The U.S. has developed a Star Ship such as the U.S.S Enterprise. The U.S. has really developed a real space ship that will function as the fictional Star Trek. The Government knew (in fact) counting on people and governments not to believe this story, if it ever comes out (a very clever plan indeed). "Space... The final frontier, this is the voyage of the starship Challenger... its five year mission to explore strange new possibilities, to seek out new life and new civilization, to boldly do what no one has done before"... There really is a five year mission to continue undisturbed and complete the S.D.I project. To avoid from the opposite side from ever finding out and even friendlier nations too, the unites States didn't even (nor couldn't) tell the families of the astronauts, and even had to make much of nothing (concerning the planned accident), thus the explosion of an emptied shuttle before the nation and the viewing media, to get the proper coverage for the world to see was conceded. The families of the astronauts could not be informed of the covert mission (understandably so) due to possible leaks to the media and eventually to the very sources the U.S was trying to keep it from. The seven astronauts are still alive and with the original mission. Praise God, the United States, the richest Nation on earth took on the impossible, although at the conclusion of its mission the U.S will have for the first time ever a defense shield that no other nation on planet earth can even compare with. Once again the United States can stand tall and proud of its conquest. It than can prove to the world that it took on alone, what others believed to be impossible and made it a viable strategic defense that will prove all others obsolete. I hail the United States, and am very proud to be part of the greatest Nation on Earth. I herein give credit, where credit is due.

God Bless America

Prejudice In A Capitalist Society

We human beings are motivated by many factors in our lives. We all (regardless of race-creed) want to be and do better than our predecessors. We want to prove the word over that we are a great people; we humans of different heritage come together for a certain cause, we can accomplish the impossible and turn bad dreams into a wonderful realities. There are masses discriminating on those of a deferent color and in summer months spend a great deal of time under the sun changing their skin color. We Americans, in the greatest nation on earth must be kind to one another, not for selfish reasons but to better our lives and that of our children. We can teach by example that we all have a common goal; to better our cause and ourselves too. Some in the melting pot are busy discriminating against those who our ancestors purposely traveled a great distance seeking and to introduce to do tasks that they couldn't do or didn't want to do. Due to those brought here from (than) strange land, this barren country came to be one of the most respected, strongest, richest, smartest, and most powerful on earth. Now that we have traveled the world over we can and must show our appreciation of our good fortune to those that helped us make this country what it is today, and who we are being discriminated against. It is up to us and we owe it to ourselves to try to make a great country even greater (first us, than the rest of the world). We humans (the best of all species) should complete the emancipation process with all those created in God's image. When the judgement day come, we can be judge by our good intentions and accomplishments, not by the color of our skin. We can overcome, but first we must work together. My hypothesis is that we will put our heads and heart together and do the right thing... I too have a dream.

Truly

Puerto Rico

Puerto Rico (Free Associated State) "Estado Libre Asociado". Puerto Rico lies between 17° 52' and 18° 30' North of the Equator, in the Tropical Zone, it is one of the Antilles Island, and its location is between North and South America and east of Central America in a vast expansion of water known as Caribbean Sea, Puerto Rico lies at the entrance. It being 40% Mountains, 35% hills, 25% plains, and has 352 types of soil. The island began its historic life as a mining island, the main product from 1509 to 1536 was gold. Three to Forty-Two million dollars' worth was extracted, which went to the Spanish Crown. Puerto Rico's size being 100-111 miles from west to east and 35 -39 miles from north to south (a rectangular shape). Total area (not including lagoons) 3,417.5 square miles. Total area (including lagoons) and small neighboring islands 3,435 square miles. The Unites States' acquisition of Puerto Rico in 1898, as a result of the Spanish-American war. The island's official name during the first three decades of American rule was "Porto Rico", it was changed to its present spelling during the early years of the Roosevelt Regime. 1917 Puerto Rico became a U.S Citizenship (The Jones Act) which replaced the Foraker Act of 1901 (the island's first American Constitution, which proved to be a political setback for congress). In 1962 it became a Common Wealth. "Estado Libre Asociado", meaning a state which is free to govern itself in its internal matters while remaining voluntary associated with the U.S only the U.S Supreme Court and only on grounds of Constitutionality can today provoke laws passed by Puerto Rican Legislature. Puerto Rico has in the U.S a resident commissions, who has a voice, but no vote. As long as Puerto Ricans remain in the Island they can not vote for President nor members of Congress. Puerto Rico in many ways resembles New York City, with its many modern Technologies. Its high-speed communications (Satellites, Telex, Telegrams, Data Radio Communications, Leased Channel, Mail and Telephones) same as in the United States.

Terrorism- Kidnappings- and Threats To Be Kill:

From watching the news T.V and reading them in New Papers it seems that if you're vacationing overseas and your American you are at risk of being kidnapped, terrorized, or threaten to be kill. It's no longer fashional being American, especially overseas (Beirut, Iran, Lebanon, Libya, and the Soviet Union. Are we to restrict our world travel to areas that terrorists agree with (agree with, so that later on they can return and take us away one by one at will)? We, the greatest power on earth are being taken advantage of (our Democracy is being terrorize). We have been kidnapped, arrested, harassed, indicted, and even killed, by terrorists, and what are we as a Nation doing about it? Even with our mighty Military, we cannot defend our people or our interests, even with our sophisticated computer hardware, with our Intelligence Departments, all our natural and National resources, cannot protect ourselves from a few craziest. Are we to give in to Ayatollah Khomeini, and or Muammar el Qaddafi? Our intelligence Departments must know that between these two fanatics (not to forget the evil empire) world terrorism is growing at a rapid rate, especially against Americans or American interests. If we don't start kicking some butt now, soon we will be locked in our homes with the shades pulled down, listening to the Ku Klux Klan while they shout and burn a cross on our lawns. We must be clear on our foreign policy and be able to back it up if ever we need to. We should be ready with the Delta Force (or similar groups) to spring into action the next time Americans or American Interests are at risk. We should and must protect our people and our Interests. We should declare war on terrorists and really mean it with action, not demagoguery, from the K.K.K to the Ayatollah and other extremists around the world. We should first prove that we mean what we say, and say what we mean...

Concern Citizen,

In respond to what some consider A Puerto Rican Problem:

The fault is not mine, though ours are the grief and humiliation. The fault lies between the warning interests of ago mighty powers. We could have been a free and isolated people in the liberty and solitude of the Greater Antilles (Caribbean) setting. Just months before American troops landed in the small island (Guánica), our politicians were successful in winning home-rule (autonomy) from Spain, than the United States acquired Puerto Rico on July 25, 1898, as a result of the Spanish-American war in a new beginning on April 11, 1899 (Treaty of Paris ratified) the United States made Puerto Rico a U.S Territory (ruled by a military Administrations (Foraker Act.). As governors-Appointed by the President(s) came to the Island, did what they could (for better or for worse) until August 4, 1947 at which time President Truman signed the Crawford-Butler Act, permitting Puerto Ricans to elect their Governors (a light at the end of a very long tunnel). We (as every other group) came to America to better ourselves, to look for work (not handouts), to make things better (as natural citizens) we thought of a better break, instead we got broken. Since we arrived we have been promised equal opportunities (so it's been said, but not done) again only meaningless words. We are not to blame for social defects, in housing, in schools, nor in recreation facilities for the labor force, this is the responsibility of metropolitan/municipal government who sometimes lack the desirability to plan imaginatively for proper provisions (when someone is to be blame for any social ills, we usually are the bureaucrats scapegoats, at every level. We have been deprived of our basic everyday rights for so long now, it's thought to be "The System" whos at fault (in many ways it is), we are not given the same equal opportunity rights that we hear so much about, we have been taken advantage of in more ways than any other group. We have been stereotyped into categories that some of us didn't know existed. The people who create these stereotype casts are also the same ones that speak of a language barrier. There may be a language barrier, due to a lack of equal opportunity. There have been professional people and reporters who because of their own problems stymy(ies) their reporting ability and reports without accurate information or figures, thus passing on the readers an exaggerated and sometimes not so truthful story. Yes, a lot has been done, but a great deal more must be done just so we as natural U.S citizens, as a people can become truly equals, and possibly benefit from the so call Equal Opportunity Fraise (Syndrome). Yes a light is clearly seen at the end of a very long tunnel, but before one reaches the other end, one must bear with every injustice, every stereotyped cast placed on us and what we do and say, and become fair game for our bureaucracies. There is always hope though, hope for a better neighborly feeling, better neighborhoods, greater appreciation of, rather than imitation of life. What I have been, does not in itself portray what I am, and certainly will not dictate what I shall be. There is always a starting point and a place of completion. I don't know which of my two countries I love more, both have its good and both have its ills. Which of my two languages, citizenship, which of my two anthems, philosophies of life, and which of two flags I care more about? It's easy to say one over the other, but deep down I think I love both equally and desperately. I only ask that the same rights and privileges be given to each and every human being on this planet regardless of race, creed, and or national origin; Than and only than can we (Humanity) accomplish great tasks and continue making this great country what it is. We than can reach for the stars and actually make difference.

P.S. In responds to the article written by Jerome James Jr., on Monday February 2, 1987

Concern Citizen

AUTHOR'S POEMS AND QUOTATIONS

1.) Utuado, Puerto Rico... Bronx, New York.... Connecticut too
Two languages, Citizenship, Anthems too...
Philosophies of life, two flags, loyalties due
From diaspora to metamorphosis completely form; from the
other tis hard to conform... J.L.T.

2.) Emancipating doldrums, Freedom and Liberty
Facsimile, Hubble bubble and lots pf trouble. J.L.T

3.) Rigid torrential cynical succumb,
Chicchic demagogue freedoms come...
Bona-fide aborigine eccentric told;
Courage, wisdom, and serenity behold,
Home sweet land of milk and honey...
Bread, butter, and plenty of money... J.L.T

4.) Planlessness, criticism, skepticism, lacking strength and
dimension, as superior or to be inferior; The symbol of an
enterprise system; War, birth, war, and growth all decay the
power concentration, demoralizing upper-status (intelligence),
creating planetary crisis, too little opportunity-jeopardizing
stability...
War, Birth, Growth and decay...
To achieve power, opportunity, strength, intelligence, and
further our capitalistic view, one must first understand its
Philosophy.... J.L.T

5.) Defenders of faith and politics, ingredients of indisputable
respect for law and judicial government...
Principles of law and public administration, representation of
a superior power well in mint...

Then turned the boomerang with anew discriminatory phenomenon,

Enthused and skeptical while descending upon Societ's dormant... J.L.T.

6.) A friend is no friend, when that friend deceives his friends.... J.L.T.

7.) There are beings who believe in belief, (God granting empty lives to search of adventure)

We, spending life making images, its sole purpose of inspiring valor in ourselves....

Hurrah.... Hurrah.... Progressive manner....

Growing up among the symbols of failure,

Passion of history, fighting for liberty, justice, rights....

Human dignity, making right all which is wrong, to help humanity become strong....

8.) Between North and South America

Surrounded by green, white, and blue

A small green island beautiful and splendor

With great country's mountain, once upon grew

Columbus' set sail in 1492

Native to the island, serenades the coqui

Puerto Rico, and Puerto Ricans history

Islands loud and clear,... America's frontier   J.L.T.

9.) Isla O pretty Isla

Borinquen soy and proud,

May god bless you, Y te guide (protégé)

In America estoy, learning democracy

Pronto to return Y estar contigo

Para siempre estar together...   J.L.T.

10.) Luck... matters not the companion

Temptation of power and glory continues embrace....

Beautiful as the stars, simple as flowers passion

Devilish inescapable, majestic qualities, inseparable

Magnetic inside look, anxiety in disgrace...

Patriot's brief triumphs and vast defeats memorable

Luck...matters not sweet victory; long live liberty.... J.L.T

11.) As I stand at the edge of earth's surface towards the sea (philosophically),
I ponder a while about events in this world all about me,
Consciously reflecting on mystic hands before my eyes, from the sea it arise
Inscribed each hand behold, words of wisdom, courage, and serenity "obstacles are many, opportunities few, success succumbs not, in part, due dignity... J.L.T.

12.) Earth, Wind, and Fire
All contribute our desire....
Quest, Victory, and challenge demands
Success awaits, if you so command.... J.L.T.

13.) This my friend you read
This my friend could tough prove to be...
Solve this riddle to catch me, and prove not so brittle,
But more to solve, this but a little riddle...
So tickle my ditto, fettle my fiddle,
Meddle in middle, and fissile brisal....   J.L.T.

14.) In the days of sail
Tall rugged ships, pirates many tales abound
For to travel freely, for spices and tar
Men willingly died for adventure, traveled afar
Temper of elements, fury caused peril
Men still sailed and drank from a barrel
These new ships, powerful, tall, and splendor
Now, men (now pirates) travel;
though gone, the days of sail   J.L.T

15.) I feel young... I feel old
I feel intelligibly superior
I feel dump... I feel human....
And will always remain so....   J.L.T

16.) Beneath a tree, A thought care to me
Employment at O.Z. wasn't meant to be....
As I write these words and look beyond.... (Must End)
A cop nears to inform I must move on....   J.L.T.

17.) We are all Sinners, or have sinned.   J.L.T.

18.) Once upon by a leaning tree
A thought, strong, clear, came to thy
As I thought (where I once worked)
It clearly came to be, known as U.S. Liberty
Land of milk and honey and sweet victory   J.L.T.
19.) Graduated from Central High
Ten years have swiftly gone by
As these words come to take meaning
Writing in my Grand Prix, by a leaning tree
A local policeman starts to lecture me....   J.L.T.
20.) If you can prove it, you got it made
If you can't Don't make my day....   J.L.T.
21.) The future is for when you want it....
Furnish he all she can
Time is short and struggle it can...
Enjoy now, while you still can
Until next future writing, will you hear from this man...J.L.T.
22.) Successfulness is being total to tour ideas.   J.L.T.
23.) I should not work so hard at staying healthy...
But instead staying healthy to work so hard.
24.) I say what I mean, and mean what I say.
25.) Dear reader of these scriptures
Frozen by time its memory it features...
Gentry and nobility I make, to better understand
Heroic memories, our country demands....
26.) Like jello, everything is penetrable....
27.) Tomorrow will be one day never again....
28.) Sneaking into darkness,
One can become unknowingly a legend, or a common criminal....
29.) Life is but a passing of generations into obscurity....
30.) A moment today, is never again tomorrow....
31.) I slept so much and for so long,
That now it's no fun sleeping....
32.) What's to become of me O Lord,
If I don't believe in you no more,

I pray to thee, to teach me right from wrong
Though my believe in you, may be weaker than strong....

33.) Love and hate as hard to define, I pretend to know
Many feelings of love or hate, I don't know...
To cherish, to love to make peace with all you know
This in my youth, I do, before I become old....
Hoping it be right, I'm sure, but really don't know....

34.) This poem my friend, goes to Lucy Ball
For many decades, we watched and loved them all....
We are saddened that you no longer will be active in- making
fun of everything around.....
This my friend, I give in tribute,
For making us laugh in your clowning around.....
(Lucy Ball died 4/26/89)

35.) This twentieth of April, may thoughts are in mind
These lines, twine and bind, just fine....
Pondering about life's struggles that become confine....
But life continues forward, while others pay no mind....

36.) From high up atop a mountain, I look down at the city very
splendor in color, rich and very pretty...
The stream's swift velocity, the suns mighty rays
A top a mountain I admire a great, small, beautiful city....

37.) Looking down from a mountain, a top New Britain's reservoir
crickets sing a song as the river descend with a roar, Resting a
bit, the climb a top the mountain I thank the Lord....
For another day he gave to us, to rejoice the liberty, - freedoms
galore....

38.) Once upon a time, down I was
Setting a goal, to write this poem, determine indeed
So read and laugh, but reflect and prosper,
Enjoy and share, intelligently....
This to be reciprocated throughout history....

39.) To want that which cannot be attain,
Is like wasting your efforts; thus end it before it begins....

40.) To want that which cannot be selected from,
Is like choosing nothing...

41.) To write without sense of meaning,
   Is like saying nothing....
42.) Working on computers,
   Is like eating a fruit from the knowledge tree....
43.) Computers are like a fruit from the knowledge tree,
   The more you look at it, the more you want to ingest it....
44.) Internal youthness is to (s) he who want it....
45.) I am now, what I'll never be again....
46.) Like a torrential river running down a hill
   Man's emotion, and capabilities should not stand still,
   As natures force due overtake, so too can men eliminate....
47.) (S) he who looks for progress shall engage in success
   Success is like taking charge of your desires and making them real,
   Success will come to all who seeks it,
   Have it? Want it? Need it? Get it!
48.) You are as pretty as the sky
   Your beauty is evermore enhanced by your intellect,
   Your charm, beauty, wit, and intellect is a welcome relieve....
49.) In search of something other than the present, now you begin to realize,
   Life is many thigs to many people, and nothing is really that simple....
50.) On hiking excursing I would sit among the rocks, and contemplate its wondrous beauty.
   Then have to entertain thoughts that this wondrous beauty might come to an end...
51.) Your lips look wonderful
   Your lips look great,
   I surely would like to have a taste...
52.) One, two and three
   Wishing success on thee
   Four, five and six
   If you can make it stick
   Seven, eight and nine
   I know you'll do just fine....

53.) May your future be bright
And your choices right....
54.) Gain from what you read....
55.) Indecision is followed by procrastination....
56.) Priority is approached by with authority....
57.) As virtual, memory is to data
The simple is that data is virtual, (simplemente)....
58.) I must get on with my life, the very one my parents have given me
Enough leisure, pondering, and wondering, now it's the future as best it can be.
No more writing, no more thinking that cannot feed me
Call for action, duty calls and now I must continue you see
Writing philosophy, thoughts of history, man's rewards indeed....
59.) From afar looking up at a river descent, I understand falling down below, with currents no one can quite command.
For many years the river roamed, roving at whatever direction it undertook.
While it usually leaves a trial behind, for its nature's way to guide this mighty brook.
As I climb farther up, to get a closer look, and a more realistic feels.
I envision the new administration with mighty powers for the environment it can heel.
This, my new year's resolution I here pronounce, to help where I can the environment in American and the world. So that in America and the world, everyone; its beauty can behold....
60.) Intelligent people do not reply on luck....
61.) Knowledge is power
Knowledge and power equals wealth,
Knowledge, power, and wealth is the answer to everything....
62.) Work your mind.
Don't pollute your brain...
63.) Beat the system with your brain power,
Not your crime rate....

64.) As spacious as earth is
It's but a little planet in the solar system…

65.) Space itself, long as it may be

66.) Must also, sooner or later come to an end….

67.) I know of everything of nothing
And nothing about everything….

68.) Is to live, to work, to reproduce and then die?....

69.) Love is sunshine on a cold, lonely day….

70.) Love, music, and a beautiful woman, makes me feel good…

71.) Treat me nice
And I'll treat you better,
Treat me bad
And I'll treat you worse!...

72.) As I look across the ocean, as far as the eye can see
Wondering what the almighty has for my future, or its really up to me,
I have worked, planned, researched: but thinking it was not meant to be,
As I study harder, work more to better my life; pleasing those who disagree,
Trying to find better solutions to life's complexities for my daughter and family
There are good times, there are bad times;
The good I compare to a symphony
If you are reading this my friend and know of a better solutions, than to you I plea….

73.) A moment pause to view a stream beneath my car, I drive by
Color of the water, pending on sun shine, varies: green, brown and I write,
My destination, relaxation, writing, philosophy, and world concerns, I confide,
Be it relaxation, recreation, or personal attention I have time, what a delight,
To a greater vista: a place of infinite size and beauty I visit dignified,
Sometimes from early to late, morning to night I come to write

Topics differ, music abound, thoughts are many and wide
As often as possible journey of reality and time of necessity I philosophize,
Now the opposite of the beginning;
A moment's pause to view a stream beneath my car, I drive by...

74.) Going away, going a ride, here is mud in your dam eye,
Hip hip horay, hip hip all ride, here is looking at you all cockeye,
Taking a cruise, going in stride with pride to riverside
I'm satisfied,
Looking down a hillside, landslide divide alongside the seaside
I cried,
The tide outside guides me inside I decide, to hide bedside fortified....

75.) Look closely at the lovely things surrounding you each day
Nature's vast beauty, diminishes; shouldn't continue to fade,
Wonderful sites, for all to joy; music of creatures of the forest serenade.
The swift displacement of nature, to better enhance humanity should not be so quick to invade...
As the so call human progress continue swiftly,
I say put constraints on this massive trade....
If the destruction of nature is continued undisturbed, sooner or later someone....must....surely...pay...
The lack of stifling this expansionist movement, nature will suffer the consequences... as surely will happen, is just what I'm afraid...

76.) Eagles sour majestically in the clean mountain air,
As their ancestors flew decades ago almost everywhere....
Today human progresses up mountains of yesterday, pushing away our symbols further away...

77.) If you have the skill,
Than, use the trade....

78.) I feel trapped in this environment, full of knowledge and desire
I feel trapped in my present physical state without any real power

One in which mental capacity does not correspond with chronologic accessibilities...

I feel in my physiology, in my neurons, in every nerve fiber within my physical and mental state trapped and not being where I'm supposed to reside and or employ....

Realizing my time period has not yet arrived; longing for that day to arrive, in which those who doubted me and my abilities would have to say:

He had a strategy, building his senses, his neurons, to where his abilities have now freed him from all the environmental constraints levied against him by the society....

I now like to do everything I know, and know everything I do, intuitively...

The power to comprehend is only to seek knowledge and master it in any way you can...

79.) My understanding of computers is like that of a computer's capabilities,
It has to be told exactly what it should know, what and when to do it...

80.) I am a lot of different people,
To a lot of different people....

81.) You should not act
According to what you hear,
But instead
Hear about how you act....

82.) Do not holler, scream, or shout about what you hear
But instead
Hear, what you holler, scream, and shout about...

83.) I go far
To be near...

84.) I said it be; not,
But be so that it is;
Could not be so....

85.) Into the belly of the earth we go
Into the forest we descent
Down, down, further we go....

Into the thickness of nature, wooded and pure we go
Down, down, further we go....
Finally, realizing the truth... There! Behold!
She was young, naïve, and for bitten for it to be
She seductively successfully sought satisfaction selectively
Being the human animal that we are, weakened by a lusty libido and temptation:
Down, down, further we go...

86.) Sitting atop a rock, looking at my reflection on water looking back
Waterfalls accumulating below in a shallow pool bric-a-brac,
Under the weather, I now feel much better stimulating my cardiac...
Such wondrous, breath taking beauty I've missed; what a drawback,
Impressive in its surroundings, magnificence, and splendor, onward I track
Imprinting on long term memory, I am sure now.... That ...
I'll be back....

87.) Butter milk (fall's) water gathering and very appealing
To form a shallow spa like pool; here I am king,
Like one's love willing to share in early spring
The site of the fall's beauty, splendor, and thrilling,
Picturesque and memorable: butter milk falls, has a great feeling....

88.) The outside world is corrupted
And corruptible
The inside world is controlled
And controllable....

89.) Feeling relax, cool, collective, and reflective at Butter Milk Falls I write,
A place of recreation for many, of all walks of life; what a sight!
Ascending the slippery rocks we journey on many occasions with all our might,
Wondrous scenery, many obstacles, pools of all shapes, and sizes, on we hike...

Birds sing, crickets sing, the water with its hypnotic affects, I am enticed

The sun shining through tall trees, short trees, trees of all shape and full of life,

Shaded areas plentiful, small caves as if to go back in time, it's all very nice.

Stress levels way down, thought processing working overtime my intellect it ignites,

Feeling relax, cool, collective, and reflective at butter milk falls I write....

90.) As the waterfalls accumulate into a spa like pool proclivity,

The white, swift, falling water thunders to complete and coalesce,

Into a quiescent, shallow, stream and visibility,

The reality at times, to clear the mind, and more room for intelligence....

M.I.A

As a watched a television on program concerning M.I.A's imprisoned in North Vietnam/Laos/ and possibly in Cambodia I was amazed that we (our government) have done so little to actually get our people back home. I write as a concern American/Puerto Rican and have to say that I don't have all the facts before me, but we should do everything in our power to get all the M.I.A's back after all we sent them over there and they did everything we asked of them.

(WE MUST DO THE SAME FOR THEM, WE OWE THEM SOMETHING)

So long as the American soldiers are imprisoned while they fought for what we believed in; people are opt to holding hostage our Democratic Ideology. I'm not degrading our great Government, in fact our Government is the very best on planet earth, and I would not trade, sell or do anything against either of my two great government, but please, please let's get our M.I.A's home. Our great government now seems to be having some problems (Irangate), what better way to redeem itself and have the American people back our great government to the fullest in whatever task it takes, but only if our people are brought home. If our great government strikes a deal, or go in and return with at least some M.I.A the people of United States will support and make our Great Government even Greater. God gave us a brain, let us put it to good use. Please put yourself in their place and I'm sure you would want to have our Government back you up, like the now M.I.A's backed up our Government in their time of need. I'm sure all the M.I.A's put their lives in what our government believed in than; the very least we can do is to get them back home, it's been long enough.

TEN COMMANDMENTS TO A
BETTER RELATIONSHIP

1.) Know your partner from birth to present
2.) Trust your partner with a questionable attitude until facts are agreeable
3.) Know your partner/family history
4.) Be as kind to your partner's/family as you would want them to reciprocate
5.) Surprise your partner and family with gifts, no matter how small, once every two or three weeks (at least once a month)
6.) Don't forget anniversaries of partners and or their families
7.) Ask for facts concerning possible (not yet) wrong doing (if at all possible make list of Don't dos- (please limit list to ten)
8.) Keep the lines of communication open at all times; respect shared is respect received.
9.) Togetherness for infinity creates a better environment for all involved
10.) Know your partners desires and weakness and try to help develop the weakness to suit your needs and desires.

CONTEMPLATING FUTURE POSSIBILITIES

I'm writing this book for a number of reasons, one of which is because I want to read in future years what my decisions were, and if I would still agree with how I went about them at that particular time. There are so many things that I would like to do and or become that I cannot make a choice. Some of those things that I, as of right now would like to do are Teach; I would also like to become a musician; I would also like to become a hoofer (I love to dance, or express myself in dance, even though I never tried to dance in public, the reason being that I was raised in a very strict religious fashion and so when I was about to engage in dancing I would feel uncomfortable and had to make an excuse not to dance); I also envision myself as a lecturer on a variety of topics. If I become a lecturer I would try to lecture by showing what I was talking about rather than just using words for people to think about. Things are better remembered when it is shown and seen how it actually works in a certain, specific way. It is better and easier to see, than it is to have to believe. I also want to become a boxer, every time I saw boxing tournament I would think myself to be one of the boxers and what I would do to win the fight. I would of course be in a better shape than my opponent and work our twice as hard, so that I could finish off anyone I was about to do battle with, in record time. I don't know if after a few years I would still do the things I said I wanted to do and in exactly the same way or if I would change something. This is another reason why I'm writing this book, to see if I will agree with the decisions I already made, how many were exactly right and possibly how many were wrong and what time period it took for them to materialize. I always thought that if a person wanted something bad enough he/she could get it, considering just how much time he/she was willing to spend in trying to accomplish that goal. So long as a person practices his/her goals, there will be some very good reasons for success, again pending on the amount of time put into making that goal work. So start that project and stay at it until you feel that you have enough of what you wanted (again the more you do it, the better and easier it will become for you to continue it) and maintain the success. I like writing about myself and things that I would like to someday do for someone else for many reasons. First because I'm always busy looking for things to do to improve society and further my own career as a writer and become more knowledgeable about things I never thought of before I became involved. I also write to see how many of my goals will actually be accomplish and in what time period. Also, so that other people who want to try their hand in something for themselves but don't know where to start, could hopefully follow these simple guidelines, and again hopefully gain success. Speaking of success when this book becomes published I promised some family members that I would try to fulfill their wishes of they told me what they were. I asked what they wanted if they were given three wishes or if they had all the money in the world, here is what at this time they choose. Carmen first choose to be a missionary, than she wanted a house and a car. Josephine's first wish was a house, then a car and finally a trip around the world. I then asked my step grandfather what he wished for and the only thing he could think of was a room full of women, nothing else. I asked my mother and her respond was for my two sisters and me to get along with everyone and be nice. Maybe after this book gets publish I will ask her again, and hopefully I could make so whatever she wants. For my step father I also want to do something special for, he has helped me in a lots of ways, but I haven't told him how, and that I appreciate everything he's done for all of us. If I ever come to a position where I could make some of those wishes come true I will. I herein mark my own words on March 8, 1978. Every time I think about money the second thing that I think about is helping other people get to where they want to go or where they would like to be in their future. I always envision myself doing something for someone else. I think that if people were given a chance a lot of them would really come through and become famous and or develop something to better mankind, but a lot of people will not get that opportunity, thus if I get mine, which I know I will, even if I have to make my own, I will help as many as possibly can. Everyone needs opportunity to prove himself. I always say that if people only take the time to think what they really want they could do it (by this I mean sit down and ask yourself; what do I want out of life? How do I go about to fulfill what I really want? How long am I going to take to acquire the intelligence (even though most people already have such intellect, but usually don't apply it) to become successful, and most important of all, am I really serious enough to put everything else in a secondary level until I get what I'm looking for? I really feel that if people take this attitude and ask themselves these and similar questions they will undoubtly find answers to these questions. Most people think and say that once you are born into a position that you are going to stay in that position until you die. Little do these people know. They have given up and are taking life one day at a time without planning for a better future. It is said that most people only use five to ten percent of their brain, imagine if people tried and practice using the other ninety-nine-five percent. I say that if people come from a poor background and really wants to take a good living and have all the extra that life has to offer, we can do plenty to accomplish just that but with a lot of hard work. The thing to do to acquire success is to put yourself in a state of mind which you will not be satisfied until you have accomplish what you set out to do. I read a book a while ago and it stated that "Most people who become rich, start out poor; when they learn the principles of how real money is made, they soon become rich". There must be ways in which people could enjoy the fruits of life but they first must find the answers to those questions. Scientists have always believed that the answers to every questions are hidden someplace all a person has to do is find out where and use it to accomplish whatever goals they want. I wanted to open my own business but didn't know where to start, until I started to put something in writing. The first thing that came to mind was renting a place (any place that was big enough to carry out what I had in mind). The second thing than was Where, and How much was this going to cost me? I have many deferent types of businesses I would like to establish. One would be a retail sales (many products could be sold), another Business would or could be a social club (a youth club, Night club, etc.). There are many others, but these would be the ones that interest me the most, the problem to open any of these businesses is that a startup income is needed to realize this goal. Something will surely materialize because I'm one of those who want it bad enough, and will make it happen.

DAYS TO GRADUATION

There are only seven days left for my high school graduation and I really don't know what I'm going to do with the rest of my life. I want to join the Marines, but it seems like that's not going to materialize. I Thought briefly of getting marry and start a career from there but I'm not sure I want to do that at this point. I fell in love with a cousin, but knew nothing could come of it because both our families wouldn't let anything serious happen between us; We had a serious talk and at the end we both decided that it was better for us all to end it as soon as possible, before it became harder to terminate, so we did and decided to remain good friends. I called her 100 miles from where I live (at her residence) and again we become convinced that it was best not to think of each other as we did because we were doing more harm than good. After this I really wanted to join the Marines and start all over again, hopefully for the better. I knew a lot of girls that liked me and I liked but not enough to make a serious commitment with. I thought about becoming a Social Worker because I like talking with youths and also like to solve problems. I also want to go to college and study as much as possible. At this point in my life I really want a career that I can enjoy and one that no one can talk me out of. The one thing foremost in my mind now is to hopefully join the Marines and really get an education, get out, after I finish my term and go to college to study hard and become someone in life. I want to also know more about the Stock Market and how to become a wealthy individual in this great country of ours. I also would like to get involved in politics weather here in the United States, on in my homeland Puerto Rico (I know that I can make a deference) if given the opportunity. I want time to go fast so that in ten or fifteen years from now I would have then what I'm now thinking of, and possibly more. I have to say that my heart is set on accomplishing these goals, I may add to them at a future date but I will not fall short nor will I cut myself out, and will not rest until all my goals listed here today, those listed previously, and those that will be added in a future date become a reality. I herein mark my own words. I would like to be a very wealthy, very important, and a very powerful person in my future dealings. I want to prove to all those that have discriminated against me personally and members of my family that even though we didn't get a fair shake, nor we were given the same opportunities that many were saying we had, I want to prove to them that I succeeded. I want to prove to my family members that I have many desires and will overcome everyone now or will discriminate against me, I will overcome any obstacles and realize all the goals I have set for myself. I'm not much of a talker in my house or any other place for that matter, not that I don't have anything to say because I do, but because "you ain't learning while your tongue is turning". There are a lot of people that don't know much about me so they speculate about me and usually they are wrong. I usually don't tell people much about me because what they think about me doesn't really interest me in the least. I want to meet deferent people and go to deferent places and do risky things, like buy gold and things that will increase in value. I have purchased ten Mexican fifty peso gold coins. I now want to know more about the Markets, as how to increase my money and possibly make a million or two. I want to invest some of my very little money and hope to turn it into a big pile. I usually save as much of my hard earned money as possible so that it can grow and hopefully have lots of it in the future. I think there isn't anything I don't want to do now or in my future, there are a lot of things to do in this great big country of ours, regardless of people's discriminatory practices, some of these discriminatory practices; believe it or not is coming from the police (right here in Bristol), The Court system, and all the way down the social ladder. The police will discriminate against others or they simply make something against us, at our court appearance the Judge will ask "Why do you think the police is discriminating against you, as you claim? Since we (I) don't know why they are discriminating, the judge always believe whatever the police says or writes down and we right away get a permanent police record (maybe that's what the police had planned all along). It is true that we have two Constitutions, two Flags, and twice as many problems as any other groups, and yes we are a scapegoat for anyone in power who doesn't have a good answer whatever ills them or their (our) community. If we all had the same rights and freedoms as every other groups this country of ours could really become much, much, greater, but until then we will all have the same problems and as a great nations we will all suffer. I hope to make changes and hope to make a big deference. I belief that some groups of people can only increase their potential in income and success by discriminating against others less able, this is their way to ensure success for themselves and their kind; in keeping less able people, showing signs of potential, in a certain level, thus they and their kind can rip in the profits and whatever success was to be attain by that less fortunate person (group).

There only remains three days to my graduation, and still I'm not sure what I want to do the rest of my life. I have added to my already many goals and desires. I would like to in some way give a T.V. presentation to motivate all who tunes in, about how one can become a better person, just by wanting to better oneself. I can visualize myself as a very rich, powerful man, one who is looked upon by all, especially by other Puerto Ricans, so that they too can try to continue to make better for themselves and their families. I want to prove my family and friends alike that I always had a desire and a vision to someday in my near future be self-sufficient and a hell of a good business man, I want to prove to all those that thought I was wasting time after I graduated from High School, even though while in school I didn't learn; after I graduated is when I really saw where I was headed and decided to change to a better place and that's when I started to really want to learn and become at everything I participated in. Like everyone else, I had to try a lot of things for myself; getting drunk, getting into fights, and trying to be accepted by my than so call friends. I in a way was never force to try pot but if I didn't than I was consider a nark so I tried it to be consider cool. I also tried pot to better understand everyone else and to better understand myself. On a psychology class I was asked by a new friend of mine if I got high, my respond was that I did but on music only. He said that a person couldn't get high on music along; I asked this psychology teacher and he couldn't answer the question, so after the class was over my

Friend asked me if I wanted to get high to see if it was the same thing or not, so I accepted and after school we came over my house, down the basement and lit up a joint, than another and another, until we had smoked eight joints before I realized I was high (he said it took a lot of rot to get me high because I wasn't inhaling the right way). I thought that a person still could get high just from listening to music, it may not be the exact same kind of high but it's a high too. I in way liked being high but the thing I didn't like was that it may me paranoid, and thus I wasn't interested in getting high anymore. I liked it because it may me relay more and see things in a somewhat deferent perspective. I want to include this experience so that if I have to talk to anyone about it I can talk with confidence and accuracy so that I can be understood on this subject (even though I realize that some people may not fully understand and think that I am an addict.) I like to date, and give a time to most of my notes so I can give specific mention as to when a certain event happened and possibly the outcome. After my friend left I went upstairs and rearranged my room over again. I lined up five mirrors (49 x 13) against one wall so that I could see my entire room and outside my window from any one position from within my room without having to look at each spot individually. If I was laying down in bed I just looked at the mirrors and could see everything in my room and out my window, so in this case pot gave me a decorating idea (that's another reason why I liked pot), it also made me feel like writing, but again the paranoia was great too, thus, the times that I may get high are and would be very limited, now and in the future. I will also give another more sobering experience that put so much fear in me that it itself put an end to what could have been a very negative role if not corrected in its proper time. I tried pot and knew what it was, and what it does in some instances and also knew a lot of people that had it as well as smoked it, I had never carried pot on me until a friend gave me some so I could hold it for him. Every time I put my hands in my pockets and touch the pot it made me feel like a criminal. Every time I saw a police car or a police I would think to myself; He knows, he's going to arrest me, that's why I was in constant fear. I didn't like the feeling for one minute and promised myself that I would never carry it on me again, after this was over. A friend of mine called and asked me if I could give a friend of hers a ride to her house, I told her I would. I picked them both up and started smoking pot on the way, than I parked so we could smoke more at ease and at the same time make out. We did and after the girls wanted to go home so I brought them but while on the way I put my window down because it was very hot, I dropped the girls home and went home; the next morning my left side of my face and neck was frozen. I mean I had no control over my left side of my face. I was really scare and promised myself that I would never again smoke pot, in the car or anywhere else. My face and neck stayed frozen for two weeks; and in that two week period I couldn't go anywhere but in my room, I had to keep the left side of my face and neck hot all the time if I wanted to rid of this problem. While I was going through this two week period I thought about what I would do if I didn't get better from my present condition. Some thoughts weren't nice, nor did I like them, but I didn't want to stay this way. I was really glad when after two weeks I looked in the mirror and saw that I had recovered in full. I now am very careful not to drive with my window open at night when there is a cool breeze coming into the car, at least not on my side. The doctors said that it was hot air retained on my body and cold air hitting my face and neck. After that I asked myself what makes people do drugs? I knew that a lot of people drank because they may want to forget something that wasn't to pleasant; but why do people smoke pot? I mean I smoked pot because I wanted to know how my friends felt and what they thought about while high, I also wanted to be accepted by them and have lots of friends. I also like listening to music while high and do other things like write, think, and see things in a deferent way while under the influence. The music sounded better, I wrote differently, and was slower and more relaxed about everything I did, but did it better because I took longer time to do whatever I was doing. I like to record tapes and records, I could really get into the rhythm. Even though a person could still reach a high without having to turn to drugs, pending on how strong your thought process are, and how well that person can control his/her mind. The magic of the mind is concentration, and knowing that it could be done, but when concentration is broken, you will lose whatever power in that thought process. The mind can be very strong, but there are also so very potent mind altering drugs that can actually make the mind think something that really is the opposite of what it should be. I tried pot in my senior year in High School, and am glad that I didn't tried it sooner. When in my freshman year in high school I wasn't interested in getting an education, I was wild. On my sophomore year I was in the same condition as the year before. One my junior year I was a bit interested in learning something but didn't push it, than in my senior year I wanted to know as much as possible, but it was near my graduation. After I graduated from high school I devoted as much time as I possibly could to reading and almost didn't smoke pot. There is one thing that I don't understand about myself, that is that I always liked school but never took any extra courses than I needed. Maybe this was because I didn't learn something that I should of. I say this because I missed two years of school. When I was living in New York City I went through First grade, Second grade, Third grade (I had to repeat third grade) but instead of going to firth, I was jumped to sixth grade. I didn't get a chance to finish sixth grade (Special Class) in New York because we moved to Springfield Massachusetts, where I started a regular Class in sixth grade and again didn't finish it because we moved to Bristol Connecticut, where I once again started sixth grade (regular Class), this time o finished it. From sixth grade I went to Junior High, and then to High School. When we moved to New York City from Puerto Rico I was about four or five years old. I remember the times we look out the window and see kids (gang member) beating each other up. One time two members of a local gang caught a rebel from another gang in our building and beat him up bad in front of his girlfriend and her mother, the mother said she was going to call the cops and the kids beating up the other kid said that if she called the cops they would kill him and put a knife to his throat. On a deferent time there were a fight between two gangs, one used to hang around the building we lived in, so they would put gas in bottles and a rag at the end, they would light the rag and through the bottles at the enemy, they would put their hands in casts (as if their hands, or arms were broken) and hit the other guys with it to do serious damage. I also remember little kids putting bottles upside down with the necks inside sewer covers so that cars go over them and break the bottles and get flat tires, the drivers would get out of their cars and chase the kids but never caught the kids because the kids knew where to run and hide. We lived in the Bronx for eight years, then moved to Springfield and lived there for about Nine Months and then to Bristol Connecticut where I did my things and finally straighten myself out (pending who you talk to). I have to say that I really like living here, but would like to take a long vacation from it and travel to other part of Connecticut. I'm waiting for the right moment. I would like very much to see the rest of the World, I would like to see every nation, every state, city, country, and every town, to learn as much from them as humanly possible. To help kids stay away from drugs and crime I would like to open a few clubs as a business for me and as haven for the kids, where they could be able to help each other and the community in the long run. I get a vast satisfaction when I'm able to help someone in their time of need, no matter how small the favor may be. I would also like to in some way help jailed juveniles I know for a fact that a lot of kids are placed in homes and that in itself destroys their lives for a long time, and possibly permanently. I would like to take them out of those homes, and jails and put some of them under my care and responsibility, so that we all can learn from one another to trust, and help where we can to make this a better Society. I would like to make for them a recreational club, take them hiking, jogging, bicycling, swimming, etc., and really help them out so they can continue to grow and put back into society what society gave them. It would be a reciprocate type of help. I would try to put in them a burning desire to succeed in the task that they would involve themselves in. I would try to get Government Officials involved, but if I couldn't realize this goal, I would go it alone. I with the help of the kids could probably become self-sufficient and it would be very nice to show a profit, this way I could delegate to the kids some responsibility so they too know and learn how to run business. I would listen to their ideas and see if that idea had any bearings to further it, and hopefully make it profitable I would like to go down in History as a great man (Puerto Rican/American), A man that would even die to help bring about a better Puerto Rican/American Society. To help people understand further both our Constitutions, both our Flags, and both our Philosophy (ies).

SHOP EXPERIENCE

This is my fifth day working in a factory and my second job since I started working. This is my first shop experience, and thus far I don't like it. So far in what I've seen working in a shop can be very boring but only if you let it get to you and that by doing the exact task time in and time out. I personally haven't gotten bore due to the many things I do. I'm a Receiving and Inventory Control Clerk and Work Distributor. I unload incoming material and sign for it, I weigh and tag the items and stock it if it's not needed for a job; sometimes I drive the company truck to deliver finish product (core) to local manufactures. I'm always busy doing something for someone. The guys in the shop tell me that after a while I too will become even more bore than they now are. The good thing that I've seen is that just about everyone working in this shop acts like if they were related (sort of). Just about everyone knows the other and some get together after work to have a beer or two, talk and socialize. Most know each other very well and show it. If something goes wrong with a machine or a worker everyone knows about it within seconds. Nothing usually happens so when something does, everyone wants to be there and help out if they can. Another thing that happens a lot is swearing, almost every other word is a swear word. When an employee swears at another employee, but it's part of the conversation. If someone from across the aisle comes over to the opposite side of the isle someone might say, what the hell you want over here, get over where you belong, you ass (these are much nicer words than the ones actually used, even though the words could sound threading, it's usually said in a sort of nice and funny way and most of the times this sort of responds is very funny, pending on your mood. The swear words used in this plant are a lot worse and more severe than the ones I mentioned above; I won't use them here because I want to keep this as clean as possible. I of course don't swear, not if I don't have to because if I do that will invite others to swear back and frankly I don't like anyone swearing at me, not even fooling around. I also don't like to horse around with anyone because someone could get hurt or they might lose their respects towards me, and I wouldn't like that either. I like to respect everyone I talk to but there are those that have to be confronted and put into their place, I've made my point clear that I don't want to fight with anyone and have heard that no one would like to tangle with me, so we usually treat each other with a since of respect. I see it this way, if we have to work together why not try to be in the best of moods and behavior towards each other, especially since we all have to work eight, nine, and ten hours every day, five, six days a week; might as well try to get along.

The work is really not hard at all but if you don't want to get bore, the name of the game is keep busy. Everything I have learned here is well learned and can be applied to improve work habits and dealings with people in general. I hope I last six months here until I'm able to retake the Marine Cor test and hopefully go into the service and make a nice career. I didn't pass the test the first time and now I have to wait six months to retake it again. My goal now is join the Marines, learn a skill and apply it to worthy career, I might even make the service my career (if I like it). I want to do something with my life. I want to be deferent from my mother and step father, I want my life to be what this great country had to offer "Many Successful Careers". I would like to travel, and do things that I like doing and learn as much in the process as I possibly can. I want to meet people and also learn from their experiences, and maybe they can learn from mine. I would really like to know for a fact that I don't have to worry about how I'm going to live the rest of my life. I want to do it all, and do what I want, without having to wait for anyone. I would really like to have a lot of money (I will have a lot of money) it might take a while to accomplish this goal but time is something I have a lot of. I would like to accomplish this goal but time is something I have a lot of. I would like to have the proper financial backing so that if I or anyone needing something, I could be in the position to make it so. I would also like very much to write a book.

In fact this is why I'm writing these notes so that later in my future I can (hopefully) put it together and make a best seller. Being an author has a nice ring to it, and becoming famous sounds even better. I want to prove that if anyone want to do something bad enough he/she can, no matter what or how many obstacles get in the way. Overcoming the obstacles is half the battle, enjoying the royalties is the other half. If I join the Marines, I would like to write a book on how to avoid war, but if its unavoidable than by all means how to win it, with no excuses, ands, or buts about it. Winning in this country is all that counts, and I more than anyone else want to win. And without any doubts I will definitely will be among the Winners. Winning is my game plan, and plan to win. I will never rest until I have realized all my goals, I may not talk about it much, but it will be foremost in my mind. I read an article in Money Magazine entitled "Discomania" it moved me in a way that I had to take some notes on it because what better way to reach the top than while having fun getting there. As I have already stated I like music and love to dance, even though I normally don't dance in public, my interests in dancing is internal. Having the soul and beat to dance is a very normal and natural beauty to watch in motion. I would like to open a Discotheque (including flashing lights, excellent stereo, the whole works). I would greatly enjoy this business, and would want anyone and everyone including me to forget all the outside hustle bustle and concentrate on fun, fun, fun, until they (I) had to go out again and start on business or had to close due to time. I would like it to be very nice, cosy, and spacious, a place where a person can go and forget everything, but what they were about to face and experience. This of course would be my personal Utopia (a world of my own, like no other) a fantasy and a reality in make belief. This place would cater to stimulating the pleasures of the brain and the body with make belief or a touch of reality, or a combination. This would stimulate the brain to the point that when a person leaves that person will be a better relaxed more satisfied, and with a since of worth, in short a better professional, with talents intact. I would ask as they entered if they can write us a message as to what we might do to make it a better or the best Discotheque anywhere. I would like to be and experience as many business ventures as humanly possible and hope to share the outcome with as many wanting to know the facts, or how we went about accomplishing a particular goal. I will work hard to accomplish everything that I have written and will try hard to help with action and encouragement and money if needed to all that may need my help, so that we all can benefit one way or in another. I will work extremely hard to earn everything I have written and things that I will write in the future, and will definitely accomplish most if not all of my goals. I respect people, especially those that respect me. I realize that I have a great many goals listed in these writings and a great deal more that I haven't yet written and maybe some may not materialize but I refuse to believe that they will not come true. I strongly feel that if I work very hard to get these goals fulfill, it's only a matter of time before they will actually materialize. The answers are there, some place, all I have to do is find them and apply them to whatever objective I want to overcome and accomplish. I will try very hard to find answers to all my questions and apply them so that all those that are with me will benefit from our search, and increase our understanding of how things happen or are made to happen, thus making this a better society, and a better place for us to live in.

WEDDING DAY

On September 30, 1978 both my sisters (Carmen and Josephine) were married on a double wedding ceremony and it was a great day. We had a big wedding party and lots of people came from New York, Massachusetts and all over Connecticut. I realized than that they now were matured enough to make decisions for themselves from hereon. I also realized and conformed to myself that the way I was dressed (in a tuck) this is how I really like to dress at all time. I actually love the way I look and feel and this is what I'm going to work hard to accomplish. I feel superior, and as if I was famous, I really feel good. I impressed a lot of family members and friends alike. My ego must of grew twice its original size, I knew that so long as I felt as I did then and now I could of gone with or taken any lady at the party I wanted to. I really didn't like going to parties because I would worry about running out of money and thus fun would have to stop, so I wouldn't have too much fun, nor would I let myself go all out in having fun. When I acquire my financial Independence in the immediate future (I can now envision myself) a very good dresser, good looking, and pleasant to be with. I will and am kind to everyone I become in contact with, but firm and fair, I would treat everyone as I would like them to treat me. The best thing that can happen what I have said and envisioned and help all those that need help in acquiring their goals. I really would help others prosper too. I have read a lot of books on how to become financially Independent. I have read books on men that are millionaires and who advices the reader on how to use their money and on where to invest it to hopefully make it grow to a hefty sum. Some of these books tell of how the author made millions in the stock market, so that through their advice on which stocks or bonds to buy and when to sell. I'm now reading books on

Successful men and how they got their success, hopefully I can follow that same road and I too might become one of them (rich and powerful). I'm now looking for an idea as to where I can invest my somewhat small amount of money and see it grow to a satisfactory level. I really would love to become self-sustain and not have to worry about money again. I think a lot about what to do with the rest of my life but don't have any ideas as to any concrete plan to follow. I'm still hoping to join the Marines, but every time I take the test something goes wrong or I'm told that I didn't pass the test, I have reached a point that I really don't know if they are telling the truth or not. I also have to admit that the test is somewhat unfamiliar to me. I was never introduced to words nor questions such as the ones in the test in any of the schools I've been to. It proves again that we are supposed to compete at a level unfamiliar to us, nor never lectured on and we are supposed to do good in areas that I never even heard of. We are the last to be educated in an equality manner and the first to get blame for civil or government ills and almost never helped to get ahead in this white control Society. I'm not bitter but I am mad as hell that discrimination is so much part of our lives, everyone talks about the minority problem, but no one talks about the minority who has made it, along with all others. I have taken the test four or five times, and even when I passed it something comes up and they can not process me. I wanted to go to boot camp as soon as possible but because the mistakes of the Air Force Officer and the Marines Officer made, I was the one to pay for their mistakes. I wanted to become part of the Marines because I felt and believed that I could really excel as a Marine, not only in the field, but also as a business man, I wanted to come out a Marine, buy a house and still compete to be the best in whatever I involved myself in. I wanted to prove my parents that I wasn't wasting my time, and that all that time I spend in my room reading wasn't wasted either. I wanted wealth so much I even started playing lotteries on a heavy dose. I would buy five to ten tickets on a daily basis two or three times every other day or so, I realized that I was losing a lot more than I was wining so I bought my last ten tickets for a while at least. There are a lot more losers than are winners. I want to invest as much as I can but in a safer place. I bought some coins from the Franklin Mint, it consists of a coin from every Nation that is in business with the United States or its allies (the entire collection consists of about one hundred and fifty coins and stamps), I will receive three coins every month for $19.00 until entire collection is received. I hope this turns out to be a good investment. On April I bought ten Mexican fifty peso gold coins, than on advice from my broker a few months later sold them and purchased twenty South African Kugerand gold coins, if the price goes up I stand to make a small sum or possibly buy a bullion (a gold bar) and so on. I had to sell the twenty gold coins because if I went to the Marines I wouldn't have time to deal with my broker, and I won't let him make all the decisions without me first agreeing with it, if I went to boot camp I won't have that opportunity. If I don't go into the Marines I would like to than go to college, but also know that my parents cannot afford to send me to college, so that may not materize either. When asked if I had any interests in going to college I would tell them (my parents) that I wasn't, because I knew for a fact that they indeed couldn't afford it. I didn't learn much while in school but always liked going to school. I will try to learn as much as I can and hope to be as smart as I possibly can, so that I can make a good living for the rest of my (and family's) life. I really hope that my future life is as successful as I now can envision it. I will work as hard as I can and not let up until these goals are realized. As far as the Marines Cor I might have to forget about it because I feel they are giving me the run around, I mean I have given the Marines a high standard in every way because the men that makes the service work are proud to have the opportunity to serve in it. If the opportunity was proposed to me, I would excel in the job. I think that the Marines and myself have a lot in common.

1.) The Marines have done many jobs in excellence.
2.) I believe that in my work force experience I have done the same.
3.) The Marines are well trained for whatever job they have to do or overcome
4.) When I'm given a job to do, I learn everything about it and than do it, keeping an eye open for unexpected occurrences.
5.) The Marines are proud men; I'm very proud myself, not only because I'm in the United States, but because I'm a very

ambitious person and love this great country which will help me fulfill my goals, etc.

I would like to become part of the Marines because like a mentioned above I love this country and am willing to fight for what it believes in, and with my help this country could be even greater. The United States is the strongest, and the smartest of all the countries on this earth... that's why I want to be a part of the Marines. In it I would feel comfortable and very effective, moving about to strengthen this great Nation of ours. In it I could make a possible career and maybe it will enable me to someday have a place in history, as so many have before. I need the opportunity and the Marines needs my services. I feel I must abandoned the thought of ever becoming part of the Marines because it feels like they really can do without me. So be it.

POTENTIAL ACCOMPLISHMENTS
FOR FUTURE VENTURES

As I listen to music and went over my photo album I'm evaluation the pictures and see if I can see in them an idea or plan that would hopefully make me financially independent now or in my immediate future so that I can start, create, and carry on, all the tasks I want to be famous for. Ever since (and before) I graduated from High School I've been reading books on Real Estate, the Stock Market, and Self Awareness Material and related fields as well, maybe I too can discover the secrets that made these man rich, and famous. I want to find a way to increase my income potential and that of my immediate family (at least those that have tried to help); I don't want to have to work in a factory the rest of my life. I want to do better than my parents have. I want to help as many people as I possibly can and all those within my Race that needs as opportunity to actually make it happen in this country. I'm looking for an idea that will make my life easier, richer, better, and smarter, to help me help others in the same way I needed help, so that we all can live a better life here, or in Puerto Rico. One thing that I would really like to do is travel all over the United States than all over Puerto Rico and finally the rest of the world, learn about other people and hopefully write book so that people that haven't done this sort of traveling can know how people from around the world live like, compare to us. I would also like to meet a sweet girl so we can share things with each other and really have a good time with all the adventures while seeing and writing about things and places in this great world of ours. I would like to create a utopia environment (I realize that many have tried and ended in failure and or in disaster) this would be one where one can live without fear of being mugged, or worse; where one can make love freely and not worry about others trying to do harm to those having a good time nor trying to steal from one another, where one can work in peace, where one can share without having to look over their shoulders for bad people, where one and his/her family can grow and prosper without having to kill for survival. I would like to be deeply in love with a very sweet girl and hope that our life is a mutual sharing understanding. I like having a good education, even if it's self-taught and to use that which was learned in a wise manner, so that others can learn just as I did. I want to know as much as possible about as many things as humanly possible about things that make this world go round, and beyond too. I would like to be a good dancer, a good looking man in excellent condition, and have an eye for fashion. When I make my goals a reality, I would never forget my immediate family, nor my few true friends. When I make it, they will benefits as well, especially if they too have a good plan for success, and needs someone to back them. I always say to myself that I didn't ask to be born, but now that I'm here in this great country, I might as well try to make the best of what there is. Materially or otherwise. I will try very hard to leave my mark in this world and still be alive to see it. I will someday be famous for discovering something of great importance, or for creating something that everyone can benefit from, or due to any of my future writings. I would also like to get involved in politics, not to say what people want to hear, and not follow through, but to do and not say what the masses want to hear. I would be my own person, I would do what I was voted into office to do, of course the research would have to suggest the choices to be right, that along with the peoples vote, it will become so. I know that I can be a leader in which I would get things done; where mountains can either make way or be removed to continue with progress, and at the same time get people involved in what I believe in. I would have the support of the people. I can also see myself as Governor of my little green Island. I really wouldn't mind to run for office in my hometown so I can do something nice for the place where I was born, in which I affectionally call my little green Island. Before I would even consider running for such a position I would first want to be asked by a large number of people to consider the position. I would like to become a very successful business man that is never to busy to talk with the very same people who voted me into office, or anyone having ideas concerning what I'm interested in or trying to accomplish, no matter who the person is, I would be well determine to set realistic goals and not let up until those goals have been accomplished. I would like to be number one in everything I do and like to be quoted by established people. I would get involved in sports, to participated or to start programs so our youths have plenty to do and thus avoid hanging around loitering in places where nothing good happens." We become that which we think about". I would start many programs so that our minds as well as our bodies grow richer and better. I would also like to make a dream car. I love to watch deferent cars and always had a goal to possibly someday make cars as a career. I would limit its supply regardless of demand. I got the idea from a magazine I was reading and came across this toy car ad. Toys can be a start to making the real thing from, even though I'm sure that this toy was modeled after the real thing anyway, but I would like to try to make a car that everyone likes and wants to drive and eventually buy. This toy car really grabbed my attention and refused to let go, thus the reason why I cannot end it there, without trying to do something about it. I personally would like to have out trying to do something about it. I personally would like to have three cars. One for riding around town or just cruising, site seeing, one for racing, and an antique for shows act. (if not) a dune buggy or a jeep, or something that would be used in any terrain. I like driving a lot and traveling and meeting people of deferent committees and see the sites. I greatly enjoy driving a car or vehicle that's fun to drive and comfortable as well. I like this car because its fast, its good looking, and no one can see inside, unless if the driver opens the Window, or let a person inside. I would be able to see people as I drive by, but people wouldn't be able to see the driver, unless of course if the driver wanted to be seen. I would built things that are extraordinary. I don't know when all this will materialize but know for a fact in my own way that all this I have written will surely come true. Those that don't believe me now will in the future either read about it or see it in person. I hope that they get a chance to see it for themselves, so I can see the expression on their faces.

I believe that a person cannot reach financial independence while working for someone else, unless you happened to work for a huge corporation and you are the president, owner, or vice president. People sometimes work ten, twenty, thirty and more years for a company and have nothing to show for. I believe that if a person starts his/her own business (being your own boss), be it building cars, or just writing about them the chances become a lot better that wealth can be kept by the originators, considering that he/she knows what they are doing and put in the necessary hours in, and really understand that business. If I go into business for myself I would know everything there is to know about that particular venture and any other related ventures. Knowing beforehand any possible hurdles or obstacles can greatly enhance your position, and financial status. I don't really see myself working for someone else, and if I do I probably won't stay working for that person (company) for very long, unless of course if they treat me in a fair manner (most companies pay a very small amount and expect a very great deal from their employees), now, I don't mind giving a lot of myself to a company but I expect to be compensated for my time and effort (I really expect fairness, and that's hard to come by nowadays, at least that's what happened in my case). The companies I've worked for have asked a great deal of me, and I have come through for them, but when I ask for an increase in pay the answer is usually NO, or the amount given is very small in proportion to work done, it is for this reason that I say that if I work for someone else I may not stay for any length of time, again if I find a company that treats me fair and is willing to pay me for what I do and how I do it than I will try to make a career with that company. When I find a company like that I will do anything and everything in my power to help in its daily operations so that company and its officials can complete, attain, and reach, with my help any goals set as a whole or for whatever Department placed in my responsibility, success would almost be assured. If I cannot find such a company (and I have my doubts) I will try to understand the Stock Market more so that I can hopefully make a living if not a fortune in it. I would love making my own decisions and not worry about anyone in a company not liking what I had to say or how I would say it. Having my own business I would be very serious and professional at all time, I would take my job and business serious and be fair with everyone I deal with. I would like to either sell or have a personal collection of coins, stamps, gold, silver, cars, etc., plenty of things that would keep me busy and entertained from the time I open the business to the time to close. I like having fun and would like sharing it with anyone and everyone around me so that time would be spent with a since of accomplishment and happiness, this way everyone produces more and looks forward to going to work every day with a since of professionalism. Not look for ways not to show up at work. I like dealing with people and in my own way always succeed in any task given me by any past employers, I like to get to know people; what they like and don't like, I also like for them to know as much about me (professionally) and my goals as possible, this way we both can better understand each other and better communicate thus creating a better work environment. I would like a job that required me to travel around the world, meeting people, see America, and possibly write a book on those travels and share them with the reading Market (public); for this reason too I keep these notes so that in later years I may put a book together. I of course hope to profit from my writings, but also hope to share that which I can with people less fortunate than me, I have a very good feeling as IF I was in love with everything that this world has to offer, even though I don't know or understand yet how to go about in profiting from its many wonderful secrets (secret of the universe). I feel that I have a lot of good ideas and that's another reason why I like writing down everything so that when my time comes I just have to go over my notes and prove to any doubter that I was genuine about what I said and believed in. I don't take anything for granted because if everything is followed through, you may discover that you are the first to either make one, write about it, or to create one for, this way credit can be given, where credit is due. I like being as informed as possible about everything and everyone around me, or that which is or could become part of me, or night concern me in one way or another especially anything to do with my business or its dealings. I like to think of myself as a shrewd business man and again know everything about that or any venture I happen to be in, or about to go into, including location, and the competitors. I would like for everyone to know that if I could help them that I would without hesitation, all they would have to do would be ask, and if I could I would, if I couldn't I would let them know right away so they knew my position as soon as possible. I realize that to get anywhere and stay on top one must know everything no matter how small the details because if you don't you're the one who will lose out in the long run because nowadays information is money and if you're not informed you lose to your competitors. I learned to be as informed as humanly possible from George Sage from Radcliff Wire, Inc., It was my job to sign for everything that was delivered to the shop, identified it, weigh it (if need to), tag it, and store it somewhere until it was needed for a job, I would have two tags, one would go with the item, the other to above person; at times I would forget where I had stocked it and he would know exactly where it was in no time at all. So knowing where everything is and about everything concerning that particular business is extremely important. At times I would try to hide a certain core from him but he would always find it in record time, than he would say to me, No problem, I knew exactly where it was all the time. I will always try to follow that example and will never forget it as long as I'm able to think and work. Unfortunately I only stayed in that shop for six months, due to not making enough, and thoughts about joining the Marines. I had more than plenty to do but not enough pay to keep me satisfied. They wanted me to prove myself to them, which I did many times over, but when I asked for an increase in pay the answer was No. I must say though that had I gotten good raise I would of really liked to continue doing what I was doing because I enjoyed it and it really kept me super busy. The only bad thing about it was the pay, and I have this feeling that other places that I might work in, are going to be the same way concerning pay. I will keep looking for a better job though until I find one.

BITTER GRAPE..........SOUR VICTORY

I wanted to write about my new job for a few days now and didn't because other things came about instead, but now that I have some times I better do it now or put it of permanently. The best way I can describe may job is Boring. The work isn't hard at all, all I do is solder two pieces of core together and feed it unto a larger spool to be stored until it's needed for shipment. When it's needed it will be uncoiled in a deferent department and put into boxes and shipped. Compared to what I used to do at Radcliff Wire, here I don't do anything. This is my third job since I started working and my second job in a shop. The pay is a little better than before but not much to compensate for the boredom, nor for the fumes inhaled, plus the work site can greatly be improved. I of course would prefer to move around and do something other than stand in one particular place sight hours a day five or six days a week for months at end and solder two pieces for core together and feed it unto a reel for storage, until it's needed. I really cannot see myself doing this for too long. I still would like to join the Marines but have to wait to Aril. If for any reason I cannot go to boot camp in April I will try to investigate my chances about going to college. I would like to further my education, even though the problem here is the cost, and I know for a fact ma parents cannot afford to pay to have me go to college so I won't even ask them. It would make things a lot worse. If I cannot go to the Marines, nor to college I will try very hard to study as much as possible on Real Estate, Psychology, and possibly political Science, even if it means books from the library, and on my own time. I sometimes envision myself as a rich, powerful Political candidate, having a good reputation and being part of upper Society with roots still deeply embedded in my original heritage. I hope that this goal will someday play a real part in my life, complete with success, wealth, and power. I really want to be someone in life, not just another Mr. Jones. I can and will become a powerful leader, I don't know if here in the U.S. or in Puerto Rico, but I will indeed overcome and Succeed, and accomplish all my goals; You wait and see. I would not let money overcome me, but instead use it to better able people to put their ideas into use and for the better man of Society as a whole. I also must mention of an unjust game someone pulled over me. It was unfair, not just, and without merit; and for that reason I have made up my mind not to accept the responsibility for its care, nor its upbring. It might have been my naiveness toward women, but now I realize that I might not trust another female for as long as I live, even though I may say I trust them. This problem will now be with me or be part of me for the rest of life. I was tricked into having an affair with someone I trusted and who wasn't supposed to have kids, of course that person was able to have kids but it was easier for her to say she couldn't have kids and seduce me than to tell me the truth and be unable to seduce me. After the affair, two weeks after to be exact, I was informed by that person that I was going to be a father; my first impression was of disbelief but the way it was said made a fast believer out of me. Things weren't going the way I wanted them to go, it seemed like I could not trust anyone anymore and I became bitter towards people in general, at least for a while. I really didn't want to play a father figure because if I did it would end my plans for a better life for me and that if my family and everything I believed in. I informed the person that I would not accept the responsibility because I was lied to plus I was used to satisfy her needs without my ok. I was involved in an affair with someone who wasn't supposed to have kids, at least that's what I was told. Since I couldn't trust this person any more I even refused to talk to her about anything, not even about the baby. This baby whether male or female would surely impede my future plans because now, the thought will always remain in my mind whether I talk about it or not, (and if I can help it, I won't talk about it0. I will feel bad about this child because I really cannot do much to improve its condition; if I move in with the mother to be I will not be fair to my ideas nor that of the mothers and would just be more problems for everyone involve, plus I would just be going through the motion of being a father without much meaning, plus my goals will become that much more difficult to accomplish. If I don't accept the responsibility (and I won't) I will never forget that I have a child and suffer the consequences alone in private, but will continue to accomplish my goals and hopefully can succeed a lot sooner than if I accepted the responsibility and played a father role. If I'm alone I feel that my chances for success are better to attain but with all honesty I think that my problems are just starting to take shape; even though no matter what problems come my way I will overcome them and concentrate on a successful conclusion to any negative outcome that heads my way. Success to he/she who seek it is all but assured. I will succeed and prosper. The answers are there, all I have to do is find them and apply them to what I want to succeed in. I believe that due to games women play, this could possibly affect my future female relationships. The way that I see things now is that as long as a girl that I'm interested in, or have been seeing shows me that she loves me and doesn't try to pull my leg on things or try's to lie about things that happened in the past will hopefully get the respect that she deserve from me. When I marry (if I do) I want to really trust that person the best of my ability and hope that she also feels more or less the same way about the things that I do. Once I know for a fact that she loves me for myself I will do anything and everything for her, but first I would test her in my own covert way to see if she's genuine about her feelings toward me and just how much she really cares for me, if her love is genuine I would try my hardest to please, not only her but everyone in her family and friends, this way we all could better understand each other and our love towards one another. I would be or try to be as good to our relationship as possible. I would show her my love in more ways than one, I would demonstrate it so she could clearly see into my heart what my true feelings are toward her and family members. She would know me physically, psychologically, and every other way, what my needs would be and what my likes and dislikes are too. I would show her my best side at all times and be on my best behavior. I will also make sure that we would have or try to have the best possible time together. Now if along the way I found out that I was lied to, than I would stop trusting and would try to get out of the marriage as soon as possible, to end any future confrontation. I like to treat people, as I like to be treated. I'm writing about this subject now because I'm going to be a father, and I want to record my thoughts here today so that later in my life I can reflect back and see what my original thoughts were. I also write this because the thought about me being a father will never leave my mind so long as I live, also because from hereon I will try not to talk about it unless if it's very important. If I ever have to reflect back on what my thoughts were on this day I will go over my notes, but I don't think that anyone is going to make me talk or write about this subject (not if I can help it). My feelings are clear to me, I just hope that I don't have to prove that to anyone. I want to say here that I really regret not being able to do much, nor look after my child, but it's because I cannot of much even if I wanted to, second because I really fool betrayed by the mother to of my child. (Lying and using trickery to try and save an ending relationship). This I think is the first time I write so much about this (usually) closed subject, but since I will try not to talk or write about it anymore I want to clear my conscience somewhat. I do feel a little better but it's for the time being. If I ever have to face my child and have to explain why I couldn't be a real father, I will just give him/her these notes and let her/him make up his/her mind, and we can take it from there. Hopefully the kid will understand my position than, and maybe continue our relationship as it was meant to be 9even though it never was); or if a relationship is not wanted I really think that I can understand that and I'm afraid I have to live with that choice. Until that day in history this subject will probably be very limited for whoever asks me about it. Another reason why this action was taken in because how can three people live on $4.65 per hour? (Less than $744.00 per month). I have changed to another job in the same shop and the amount is more than I was making before. The climb on the so call Social Ladder is harder and harder to climb, but a necessary one. The steps get further away on every step I climb onto, even though I'm making some small progress. I'm now a Grinder and hate it even more than soldering but I need the extra money. I have one week more before I have to take the Marines test again, this time I'm more confident than ever before and really want to go in the service, I really want to get away from these boring jobs. Since I graduated from High School I've been doing a lot of reading, mostly on Real Estate, (How to make big money in land). I have also been saving as much money as I possibly can. It seems that now that I'm out of school I'm studying more than when I was in school. Now things are much more than when I was in school, the feelings are deferent, people seen deferent and everything is more serious. I have been buying Government bonds and hope that I join the Marines so I can buy about six hundred dollars' worth of bond. In the Marines I can save all my money, study as much as I can, and learn a skill, which can be put into use when I get out in a few years (if I don't make a career in the service). In later years from now I can reads these notes and see where I was right, where I was close and (heaven's forbid), where I was wrong, if so by how much. I would really like to make this into a book, hopefully a best seller, so I can put into effect all my goals, I can than plan my work, and work my plan. I want to write a book so I can show the readers just what I had to go through, how unfair life can sometimes be and despite all this how I grew to become an author, rich, and powerful. And most important to show them that if I did it, than they too have a chance to fulfil their dreams, all they have to do is try and don't stop until it becomes true until it materializes into fact. We all can better work to improve ourselves and Society as a whole.

BOOK

For a long time now I've been thinking about writing a book, but don't know how to start or what subject to unite about. Just about this same time a Real Estate Agent called me to ask if I was still interested in a parcel of land I once asked about. Then it hit me, why not write about Real Estate. I mean now that I'm getting involve in buying land I might as well write a book on my purchases and its conclusions. As I make a purchase I would describe how I found out about the parcel or whatever property I happen to be interested in, and how I will paid for it. I will keep notes on how the transaction turned out whether I have any unforeseen problems, what I do to solve them, who I may have to higher to do things that I cannot do myself (Title Search, etc.). I will keep doing this until there is enough information to actually write a book. I would write according to however the deal turns, and will record it immediately after it happens for accuracy. This all started on April at my sister's house where she gave a birthday party in my honor, I thought to myself that if I was looking for land to buy and found a lot in Plymouth, Terryville, in Fall mountain (Eastview Road) for $3,000 plus the sanitary assessment which was $775 upon taking title to said property (I had a clause put in, stating I had ten years to pay for it). The property itself is 16.6 feet by 165 feet by 32 feet by 110 feet by 108 feet, an irregular shape. Lot # 19- Map #91 lake front building lot. Due to the lake I thought it had a lot of potential for increase in earnings, and to keep myself in shape while I did things to improve the wooded let. One can also go swimming in the lake, once can canoe or fishing, or who know what could be done in the lake, there can be a lot of recreational activities to do, or cheat due to the lake. I like the property and look forward to continue buying parcels, and hopefully a house in the very near future, and make a small fortunes in the process. I hope this is a good start and that I can make a living on this venture. I don't plan to sell it anytime soon and possibly hope to build a house on it. I look forward to knowing the ins in this vast field, however complex it may be. Knowing everything there is to know about Real Estate can really help anyone wanting to know how to make it big whether in financial turns on in building inventory. The information alone is enough to keep anyone busy for months or years at a time, not taking into account the time that one must put into the actual property itself, checking to make sure that you get what you paid for. There is a great deal of information on this subject and I will start by reading every book I can find, than I will put into effect what knowledge I gained and hope that it turns out for the better.

FUTURE HOMES

I think to myself that when I become a millionaire I would have to customize my own house because no one would really know what or how to draw up the plans for my many dream homes. I will list all the homes in this section so that the readers can better appreciate the deference in styles and its complexities, and how they vary. I think that only I can see in a mental state how this and other houses will operate, and how it actually looks. I want an elevator to be able to get to the second level while still on the first floor. The first floor will be ground floor, an elevator ride onto the upper stage (the only way to reach this floor is only via the elevator) and the elevator will fit perfectly into the opening leading into this second stage. A pipe, like the ones used in fire house to go down in case the elevator break down and someone is in the upper stage could use in emergency cases (obviously this can also be another way to reach the second stage on the first floor). On the second stage in the first floor I would like my study, a library, T.V. monitors to keep track of the entire grounds outside and inside, and a pool table for relaxation, a mind computer system for outside communications, and possibly a short way radio, also for communications sake. Than upstairs in the second floor I would like the Master bedroom (very fancy), a music room (stereophonic), a small movie room, large T.V. screens, and a small pool to relax the muscles and release tension. On the first floor I would like four to six guest rooms all fully equipped with all the essential amenities, the kitchen in a nook and a large, half recreational room and half weight lifting room with T.V. and music capability. All the doors to each room can only be open by me; There would be an opening by each door on the wall where I would put my hand (arm) and due to my physical chemistry and or body temperature the door(S) would open, the person enters and doors closes. To exit from the inside a person would just push a button on the wall and door(s) will open automatically. Since every person's physical chemistry is deferent and no two are alike no one can enter a room without my help or if someone is already inside a particular room. Security would be outmost in importance in all my homes, be it for my personal use, or for sell. I really believe that with price not being an option an electronic device can easily be installed in walls with doors so a person can stick his/her hand into it to get door open and do exactly just that, if the physical chemistry isn't what it should be than doors will not open or a handcuff device can automatically look that persons are (hand) in that position until someone can come with a code or in authority and release that person or make an arrest if that person has no business being there. The physical Chemistry is not the only way to determine if a door opens or remains closed; again body temperature is another form to gain entrance or make an exit, possibly the hand (arm) could be moved while going into this opening, and other factors as well. I would of course involved myself in many activities to possibly share this technology with other people wanting the same amenities (maybe at a cost, but this would be to create jobs) and stimulate the economy. I would also like to participate in sports, teenage programs, swimming, mountain climbing, horseback riding, etc., I would really be active in many things and with a lot of kids and their parents and help out needed organizations, anyone who needs us or my services and if their cause was for a good cause. I would either ask my parents to come and stay at my house or if they preferred built one especially for them, the way they wanted it, the same would apply to both by siblings and their families. If they choose to stay at my house I would built their rooms for their special needs, complete with everything imaginable, and still have enough room to move freely and relax without having to go anywhere for fun, unless if that's what they wanted to do. I would live well, and all those that at one time or another even helped me in any way, shape, or form for any reason would be rewarded or helped. I would help anyone I could, with advice, money, or in any way I could that wasn't illegal. I believe that I can make a deference and when my time comes I will prove what I have been writing about. I would try to create jobs, and plenty of tidings to do so that everyone can participate regardless of color, race, or creed. The name of the game would be stay busy, creating things to do, and staying happy, and share everything possible with as many people as humanly possible. To better understand each other, and better fulfill our dreams and that of others. I really look forward to make all this come about, and as soon as possible. To then I'll see you there.

Spinning Bed

The bed frame would be mounted on an adjustable base that would rotate when the rotating button is pushed. The base in similar to those used in auto shows to show the car from every angle, without having to move the car. The base can be electric or battery operated, and would have wheels for easy movability.

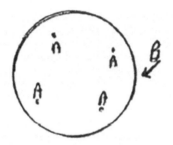

B=Base (could be round or square).
A= Wheels for easy movability

I would like to also build a house that its rooms would spin around so that no matter which room any members of the household be in, they would be able to see the entire grounds. The inside would have the capacity to rotate, not the outside of the house. Each room could be made to rotate individually or the whole inside, pending on how many buttons are pushed at the same time. Each room would have its own button to either be use or not.

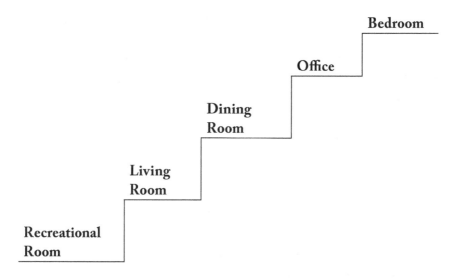

The house itself would be unique and revolutionary per say. Each room would be built in the form of steps, and each room would be higher than the other, as seen above. The size of each room would be the least of any possible problem. If a member of the household was in the recreational Room, that person could be visible from every other room. Regular stairs can be used to get to the other rooms, an electronic solid curtains can be used as doors in time of privacy, either coming down from the ceiling (and having a door large enough to have one person exit or enter), or closing from either side of the walls. I have many deferent plans in which houses could be built with a limited amount of money and the style would be very impressive. If I was the one to build these houses I would also decorate them, and act as the renting or selling Agent and or the Property Manager to avoid the problems that usually go when more than the common parties are involved. The shape of each room could be deferent pending on what the people who would occupy the house (apartment) wanted. The shape could be made by deferent wall sizes. (example) a wall could be erected in the middle of a room to make it two small rooms within a room. The walls could also be made in deferent shapes and sizes, all to sult the needs of the occupier, and all at reasonable expense. All these houses (apartments) would have enough closet space; and if expense was no option the ceilings and the floors could be lighted (lit), and possibly have glass floor that lights up.

Again all very unique, and revolutionary. I would like to be the one to find a way to solve poverty. I still to this day have a lot of ideas, but find it difficult to establish an objective that would result in wealth or fame, but have not given up hope, nor will I give up until some of these goals (if not all) materialize. I will exhaust every possibility I can think of, and if still cannot find success, I will start looking in a deferent area and start all over again, until I succeed in what I seek. I really don't believe nor feel right when either I or a person gives up in despair after trying to overcome a possible problem or a challenge. After a person overcomes a challenge or solves a problem the rewards are that much sweeter and better. In my future home, I want an octopus shape house (mansion) with eight to ten legs (possibly changing attitudes from low to high, on lifts). On each leg would be a large comfortable room containing many amenities to please the occupier. In one room there would be a full size computer display (all the walls would be mirrored so I could be able to self-analyze those in the room as well as myself), pool table, spa, T.V., stereo, large library. My desk, phone and an alarm system to protect the entire Estate, grounds and all. In another room there would be all the above plus a movie projector, pinball machine, big T.V. screen, and it would be sound proof, so noise wouldn't be a problem to the rest of the guests in the house. In another room I would have an indoor pool, weight lifting machines (recreational room) all types of games. In another room would be my second and the best investigative office with computers, phones, all connected to the stock market (?) and travel services, this would be right next to the first office so that if ever needed to open both together would create huge communication center. In another room would be a small science lab and other things to experiment or create things or for information gathering. In another room I would like to show my coins, paintings, stamps, etc. (a mini museum) to exhibit these items. It would of course have its own alarm system. I would like to also have a secret room where most of the house could be viewed without being seen, for security purposes. Of course there would be enough bedrooms for members of the household and any guests that they or I invite. There would of course be dining room, another recreational room for smaller kids. I would like the shape of this house to be very unique. For this goal to materialize I of course have to be very wealthy. I would like to become the richest man in the world, so that I can do whatever I want to do, when I want to do it and not have to ask anyone for permission, nor have to wait for things to happen, instead I would be in the position to make them happen. I would like to know as much about our Government as humanly possible, and other governments as well. I also really like to know about the stock market, and what makes the world go around as it does. Knowing and understanding everything around you is what makes people what they are in this great world of ours. Information in part is what makes a person wealthy; thus I have started acquiring as much information as possible, so that I too can become wealthy, even the wealthiest man on earth. Hopefully this goal will certainly materialize in the very near future. As a wealthy person I would try to create jobs for homeless people and give them a new hope. I would also try to create things for problem people or people in general to do, challenging things, such as a new game. Shoot a color bullet and let participants try and find it, this could give people the freedom to work or create technology and apply it to finding a tiny bullet. The person or group that finds the bullet would win a prize; maybe someone can create a technological breakthrough and create an item that can follow the bullet from the time it was shot until it was located. Maybe something even smaller could be found, by one of these invention(s). Our technology could be improved thus we all could continue to prosper at a more rapid motion. (Manner). Another possible idea, to build homes in the future would be to build them in ground. Houses could actually be built underground to better enhance the energy situation, and safer during earthquakes, and a better protection in case there over is a nuclear explosive energy release, due to accident, or to war. The last part of this statement may sound ill nature or illogical but it must be taken into consideration due to the cold war words between both super powers. The closer and or friendlier both super powers become, the likelier the possibility of something going wrong, and in a rash moment an entire race and its lifetimes work could be wiped out; those that are better adapted within the environment stand a better chance for survival. I'm not trying to scare anyone into anything, but so long as the possibility exists, one must at least acknowledge the facts. Having said that I should also say that we should I work hard to make a better world for everyone to live, learn, and progress in, to better understand each other and really make this a better world to live in. My idea of living life is to live it to the best that society has to offer. I'm trying through this book to inspire people in both my countries and in both hemispheres to hand together to discover new ideas, to improve old ones, and to expand our mental capacity so that we all can progress from our research, and give our children a better future. There are a lot of new ideas to become exposed, and an equal amount of old ones to be updated, and a lot more to be done so that knowledge can be acquired by anyone who wants to know, not only for those who can afford to know. With a little work and some creativity we all can become greater and share in this wonderful dreams; (by making it a reality).

SECTION 2

THERE IS NO LUCK
IN SUCCESS

CHAPTER ONE

THERE IS NO LUCK IN SUCCESS

Success- The favorable or prosperous termination of attempts or endeavors; the satisfactory accomplishment of something attempted; the attainment of wealth, position, or the like; a successful performance or achievement, A thing or a person that is successful. No doubt that once you decide to succeed, there is no way that you will not get to where you want to go.

As you make your attempts at a higher level, you can reflect back and see the progress you have made. That is when, you are in a better position too. The satisfactory accomplishment of something attempted. Again here is when you have accomplished the first step, and once in a while you make a mental picture of what you accomplished (this mental picture will motivate you to want to try again hopefully at a higher level).

The more you attempt with the thought that you will succeed, without any negative thoughts in mind, no doubt you will succeed. Last, but certainly not least, the attainment of wealth, position, or the like. Now on this step; some people might call it a stage, since you know that you could do anything to go wrong, I will take my time doing it; here is when you start to slow down a bit, right here is the most important and crucial moment because if you accomplish this step without hesitation or slowing down here is where wealth might come in, and here too is when you acquire a position as well. When you know that you have accomplished this last one, then you know for sure that there really is nothing that you cannot accomplish. Everything is at your fingertips. The answer is there, all you have to do is find it, and when you do is when you will successfully perform and or achieve. Then you are known as a person that is Successful. Eureka! Eureka! (I have found it! I have found it!)

When I am dead, I hope it may be said: "His sins were scarlet, but his books were read."

This book was publish for many reasons, one was to prove to those in doubt that if you really want to, you really can, and here is proof. I also wrote it because I like writing for personal satisfaction, and do something positive for Society, my family, and for myself as well. I wanted to share with everyone that which I learn am learning, and that which we all can learn, for the better of human kind and society as a whole, worldwide.

There are those that stereotype others to only certain capabilities and really underscore what they themselves can do. I have been told that due to my background I should not try to do too much because I either didn't have the proper education or I didn't know what I would be up against. When I hear people talking in this minified manner it tells me that they themselves have and are making less of themselves than they can do in reality, and thus they think small or with impossibilities. I am always thinking in terms of making something for the better of men kind as well for my own interest and personal gain. This is the American way.

Financial Success

All the material in this book are first hand, everything was noted down for accumulation and for accuracy especially for this chapter. As of May 3, 1979 I started considering myself a Property Owner. I knew it was not a very big investment, but I had to start somewhere and get the necessary information and experience to fully understand the Real Estate field and its dealing as a whole.

The down payment which I made was********************************$ 500.
The purchased price was***************************************$ 3000.
Assessment of severs was*************************************$ 775.
The attorney's free were**************************************$ 175.
Total amount paid at closing***********************************$ 3450.

The cut down forty-three trees over a six year period and on September 16, 1985 I sold the Lot (The parcel of land now looked much bigger and a lot better) The property was (is) located in the town of Plymouth, County of Litchfield and State of Connecticut. The parcel designated as Lot # 88, Section 5, Bounded as 105 feet North 32 feet East 101 feet South and 16.6 feet west. I sold the lot for $ 11,500 and was (am) very happy about it and the experience and information I acquired from the exchange. I have included as much information about this Financial Successful experience and about all the Employment positions that I had since my first job back in Stop & Shop, starting on March 1, 1976 until July 17, 1978.

Page 4 will entail with accuracy my Employment History and you can see that pending on what you want to do you really can do it.

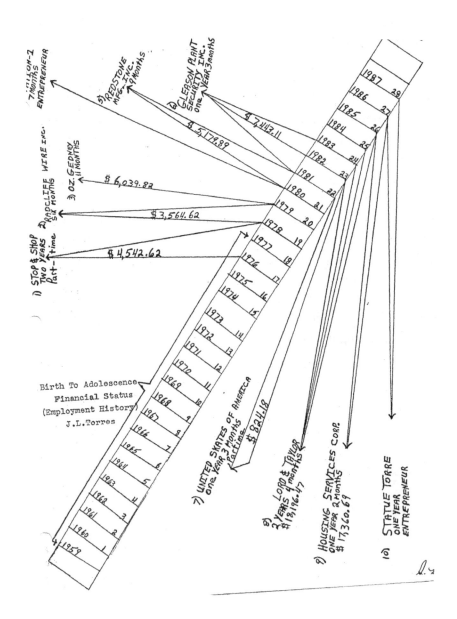

Birth To Adolescence
Financial Status
(Employment History)
J.L.Torres

1) STOP & SHOP TWO YEARS Part-time

2) RADCLIFF WIRE INC. SIX MONTHS

3) OZ. GEDNEY 11 MONTHS

4) REDSTONE MFG. INC. 9 MONTHS

5) GLEASON PLANT SECURITY INC. ONE YEAR 3 MONTHS

6) TILLON-2 7 MONTHS ENTREPRENEUR

7) UNITED STATES OF AMERICA ONE YEAR 3 MONTHS Wartime

8) LORD & TAYLOR 2 YEARS 4 MONTHS $18,196.47

9) HOUSING SERVICES CORP. ONE YEAR 2 MONTHS $17,360.69

10) STATUE TORRE ONE YEAR ENTREPRENEUR

$2,443.11

$5,178.89

$6,039.82

$3,564.62

$4,542.62

$8,241.18

CHAPTER TWO

SUCCESSFUL PEOPLE AND HOW THEY BECAME SUCCESSFUL

In Chapter one I described how to attain Success and the person that wanted to attain it. Now in this chapter I will talk about the Successful person and how they go about acquiring more of what they want (Success, Fortune, and Fame.)

Of course different people measure success in different ways. One person might say, and feel that as long as they have a lot of friends and a place to stay, they are successful; yet others might say, all I want to consider myself successful is a million dollars. Others might say that for them to consider themselves successful they must have a lot of money as well as friends and a nice house. Successful- Resulting in or attended with success, for many people this might mean trying to accomplish something that they already know how it's going to turn out.

My meaning is to try to accomplish something regardless of consequences. By this I mean that if you try to do something that you don't know how it's going to turn out, than you try harder because if you don't, you might not get what you want, even though if you try for something extremely hard and don't succeed, at this moment don't think in a negative way, but say to yourself well I tried it that way and it didn't work.

What if I try it this way? I guarantee that if you don't stop and think positive after you fail, you won't get to where you want to go. The thing to do is get back up as fast as possible while you are still remembering it well, and start all over, but this time when you get to where you failed the first time, you won't let it happen again because you would take a different approach. Now after you take a different approach and you don't fail again, you have succeeded; if for any reason you fail for the second time don't worry to much because you can try again and again until you accomplish what you are interested in or what you want to be in. if you succeed the first time "Great", but don't say or think that you were lucky because you were not; you made it happen.

You can say to yourself, I'm going to succeed no matter what, here you are thinking in turns of success. You can and must proof your ability, you must show the desire to take an unsuccessful task and turn it around into a Successful enterprise. A successful person enjoys and id ready to engage in undertaking of difficulty(ies), risk, and or danger. One who is ready to start and carry on untried schemes with the thought that he/she will succeed. This does not mean (I hope you don't interpret this to mean) that you will always will succeed; however if you have the proper information and the right spirit you will undoubtingly attain success in that field. I once again must bring to mind that there are those who not do, and not let do, there are those who fight, but don't like might. I can only suggest that success is for the best, or for those who take the time and make something of it. There are a lot of people who are too busy to try for a better life or a better career or a higher paying job (too busy shopping, hanging out with their friends going out every day, or just staying home watching movies, or TV.) This does not mean that if you do what I just mentioned above that you won't be successful. If you are always shopping, maybe you can become a professional shopper. If you are always hanging out with your friends, maybe you can do something for the better of (for) the community. You can form a neighborhood block watch and be the very best at doing that. If you go out every day, maybe you can think of a good idea that you can put into effect and make income from that. If you stay home watching movies or TV, maybe you can practice how to act (maybe become an actor/actress) or become a model, sure all you have to do is practice, than you can show them what you can do. If you mean good, you will find a way to make, event, create, or change something already in existence and make it better. You have the ability to actually make the difference. You are unique, intelligent, able and capable of many accomplishments, but if you are one who is always busy doing nothing or being invaded by your peers doing drugs or consuming alcohol or sex than you might not see the point of view of this book; yet if you are in one of those category (ies) you can still change for the better and become a major success; if you want, try and see for yourself. The thought is, do you really want to. There are a great many of us in this overcrowded wonderful planet of ours, but together we can make it a better place for all of us to live in (we should live, and let live) we as a race do make the difference. We can survive anything, we can adopt, we can read, we can write, we can think, we can imagine and envision many things, and most important we can put all these things into effect and succeed and prosper. We are the smartest beings in this universe; let's work together to make this a better would in which to live and enjoy its amenities. What I'm saying in this chapter is that with the proper motivation and some knowledge we can accomplish whatever we think of (whatever we think of in turns of doing for ourselves. If we don't have the proper motivation, we can seek it, we can shape it, we can make it grow and most important we can use it, and please don't let go! Have faith and it will be done. Enjoy that which is around you, be happy and share it. Be creative, positive, and enjoy success. Learn all you can. To be the success that we all want to be, we most use the other 90% of our brain. Most people only use 5% to 10% of their brain. If you really want to be a successful person and you want to do something to prove it; before you start, it would be a good idea to sit down in your desk (room, or any place where no one can disturb you) and start writing about what you want and how you are going to acquire it. After you have finished writing what you want and how you would go about in getting it; write down questions can you can later answer. Questions such as:

1.) Do I really want what I have written down?
2.) Am I really interested and prepare for this task?
3.) Would I start but not finish this task in which I'm interested in? (Would I go half way, than turn back or quit?)
4.) How bad do I want this goal?

5.) How long am I ready to spend on this goal?

6.) Most important, when should I start?

I think that if you ask(ed) yourself these questions and the ones that you have, you will be on the right road. "You will be on the road to success". Achieving or having achieved success, here most people say well, I have done this and that before, so I must be successful; fine but the way that it should be approached is to as soon as you accomplish one goal set another one and continue the process until you feel like you are at where you want to be. Here you would have a lot of confidence in yourself, because you could look back and see all the goals that you already have accomplished and the ones that you want to accomplish next, here you start to actually do something about it. You will go at it with a greater desire because you will know what success is and how it feels to be successful. The good part here is that you are out to better yourself and your ways of being and acting, you will have a new way of looking at things and your own since of accomplishment. When a person tries to better himself/herself, they are on the road to a successful life. You are going out to achieve something; You might not know what but you are going to try hard, if not harder than before. When you have succeeded in obtaining wealth you would be in a very good position. You will be recognized as a very successful person. So if you want to be successful, you not only will get there but you will also get income, power, and the recognition that goes with success.

CHAPTER THREE

DREAMS AND SOME INSPIRATIONAL QUOTATIONS

Big Dreams. Most people are so busy trying to earn a good paycheck that they never actually make any money. Some think they are happy but never think about exactly where they are at or where they want to go. Find out how much money you feel you are worth and make plans to fulfill them. "Plan your work, than work your plan". Don't just work eight hours; get one full time job and one part time. There are three eight hour shift in each day. You can sleep eight hours and still have sixteen to work (even though some people's work is not really work) "D.J.'s, Actors, Musicians, etc. The main concern is to know what you want (really want), and how to go after it until you do it, or get it done. If you have the motivation to do something you want or like but don't know how to go about it, just start anywhere. Example; I wanted to find out about diamonds and how people sell them and who is interested in buying. I didn't know what to do or where to go for information, so after a few minutes of thinking about it I decided to go to a jeweler and ask him/her a few questions. I went in to the first jewelry store I saw and a gentleman asked me if he could help me; I told him that I had a thousand dollars to invest and thought a diamond would be a good choice. First, he agreed. Second, the information I received first hand was very useful. Of course I didn't buy the diamond and I wasn't going to buy it, I just wanted the information. The point here is that when I started out I knew absolutely nothing about diamonds, and when I left the store I had a very good idea of how they were cut, who sells the most diamonds in the world, and who controls the amount of diamonds being sold, and a lot more. Now if I wanted to know even more about diamonds I would have gone to another jeweler, or have found other means. When you want to find answers to something, you can very easily find them, even by asking people that know nothing about the subject. The thing to do is ask questions and try to get answers to them. Never ask one person for his/her opinion about something and believe everything he/she says as fact, even if he/she is a professional. He/she could be one hundred percent right; but he/she can also be wrong. Instead, ask as many people as possible. It is always better to get at least three opinions from three deferent individuals, than the old fashion way of believing just one person. Ask as many people about what you want to know; the more people you ask the more you will know and profit from it, also if at all possible you should invite two or more people over and present your ideas or whatever you are going to do or what you want to do and get their opinion (it might be nice if these people were friends). Criticism can help at times; maybe one of your friends can give you the answers to your questions. Try to form a group so that they can hear your ideas and you can hear theirs. After everyone has left, think about what they said than reverse it completely to see if it makes any sense. The point here is to think about every detail presented, whether good or bad, maybe you can find the bad ones and correct them before they happen. After all if you don't catch the bad ideas before they go into effect, they can cost you dearly.

"I had Ambition, by which sin the angels fell; I climbed and, step by step, O Lord, Ascended into hell". – W.H. Davies. Intellectually I know that America is no longer than any other country emotionally I know she is better than every other country. The United States is not a nation of people which in the long run allows itself to be pushed around. "What I aspired to be, and was not, comfort me. –P. Browning, Rabbi Ben Ezra. . . ."

A man must not swallow more beliefs than he can digest. – Havelock Ellis . . . .

"We demand that big business give people a square deal. – Theodore Roosevelt . . . "Not what we give, but what we share, for the gift without the giver is bare. – J.R.Lowell . . .

"God offers to every mind its choice between truth and repose. - Emerson . . .

"Civilization means a society based upon the opinion of civilians. It means that violence, the rule of warriors and despotic chiefs, the conditions of camps and warfare, or riot and tyranny, give place to parliaments where laws are made, and independent courts of justice in which over long periods those laws are maintained. – Winston Churchill. . .

"I came, I saw, I conquered. – Julius Caesar. . .

"See the conquering hero comes sound the trumpets, beat the drums. – Thomas Morel . . .

"but if I'm content with a little, enough is as good as a feast. – Isaac Bickerstaffe . . .

Culture is "to know the best that has been said and thought in the world". – Matthew Arnold . . .

"The great are only because we are on our knees. Let us rise! – P.J. Proudhon . . .

"But be not afraid of greatness: some are born great, some achieve greatness and some have greatness thrust upon'em. – Shakespeare . . .

"A little nonsense now and then is relished by the best of men. – Anon . . . "Let us have faith that right makes night, and in that faith let us to the end dare to do our duty as we understand it". – Lincoln

CHAPTER FOUR

CONQUERING WHAT YOU WANT OUT OF LIFE

This book was written to give you an idea about the things that you want to do. If you want to do something bad enough you will not only conquer it, but you will also profit greatly from your persistence (To continue steadily and firmly in the pursuit of any business or course commenced; to endure; to be insistent. In wanting to do something bad enough you should always "plan your work, then work your plan." This way you have a guide to follow. Again this book was not written to show you how to go about doing what you always wanted to do (even though it states ways that you should follow to help quickens your pace for a successful conclusion in the field you have chosen.) but to stress that you can indeed do it. If after you finish reading this book; you have an idea or a though, write it down someplace in the Notes and Thoughts space provided at the end of every chapter, and with time on your side you can look up the information or anything you want to and perfect it to your liking. (example- read this book- chapter by chapter and at the end of every chapter write what you think about it, write down if you agree or disagree with what your reading, whether you would write it the way I just did or how would you write it. You might say, I liked it because: : : It made me realize that I can do anything I really want to do; or you could say well I didn't like this chapter (book) because it wasn't worth the six dollars it costed. If you really want to know everything about the book or the Author you can read it a second time, this second time look for things that are close to your own liking or disliking. Write down the way you felt immediately after finishing that particular chapter. The point here is that after you read the book two or more times you should really know a lot about what is in it, and maybe have enough notes to actually write your own book.

I might have said something in chapter one that you could make clearer than I did; or you could have written more than I did. You can even read this book one page at a time and write two or three pages worth of notes that you were taking (writing), and before you know it, you have written your own book. I have found that by reading a book two or more times and taking notes on it, you can learn a great deal more. I would read a book once, then after reading it, depending on what the book was about; I would write about three or more pages of notes. I would read it again, this time I would write about one, two, or three pages per chapter. This would make me remember the book more clear and what it was all about, plus I (you) have written the things you like and disliked. If one or two years later you come across a matter that the book made sense in you don't have to read the book again because you can just look at your note; or if someone asks you to help him/her. He might think that you are an expert on that subject, and in a way you are, because you know the good things about the subject as well as the bad things (if there are any.) You could advise anyone and point out the dangers of a matter and the advantages of it too. The more you know about something the more you understand it and how it started or how it might end, and more important, where it's going, or how much it will cost. Information is sometimes greater than any amount of money. Information- News of intelligence communicated by word or in writing; facts or data; knowledge derived from reading or instruction, or gathered in any way; A quantity which measures the possible numerical uncertainty in the outcome of a particular experiment. I want to point out that all you need to succeed is really a burning desire and a must accomplishment attitude; by this I mean that everything you see you should think in turns of making it better or trying to make it easier. I hope this is not interpreted with any illness. There are those who always think negative, the doubters, the ambulance chasers (however slick and deceitful they never believe in others or themselves.) You must think that you can accomplish anything put before you and much more. If you are not working for yourself the Company you work for may stifle your desire for success by either the pay issued you are by stereotyping your ability to perform. There are those (in key positions) such as Company Presidents, Supervisors, Foremen, and the like that are trainers of associates (employees) and either don't know or can't see an associates ability to accomplish tasks thus when that associate confronts him (Supervisor) about the lack of income or promotions; the supervisor may say something like: The leadership trait is the core of the individual's maintenance of an effective worker role and advancement to a status in the work force-; I as your supervisor have not seen your performance increased to warrant either an increase in income or in a promotion. Others may say something like: All new employees shall be evaluated at the end of thirty days trail period, and there after annually on the anniversary of employment. The thing here is that if you check the facts; someone other than you, like the supervisor's friend does have what it takes to have that very important increase or that promotion. I'm not saying that there are those associates that deserve an increase in pay or a promotion because I realize that some don't deserve it, but there are those that work their butts of and the supervisor(s) don't care or don't know so an increase is not given. It really depends on the Supervisor who gets what or who gets nothing, if you find yourself in the position; speak to your supervisor and inform him/her that you are willing to work hard to be able to receive an increase or a promotion. (This may and may not get you the increase but at least you are trying, and you took the first step to your advantage.) You won't lose anything by trying, but you stand to gain (pending how you present the facts to your supervisor and speak to him/her.) If you still don't get anything as is usually the case, keep trying from time to time. The thing here is to continue working just as hard as before (or harder). Continue the quest, the search, the challenge to success. Remember that if you really are unhappy about what you're doing at work, you really don't have to stay there, you are there because you want to be there. Do what you really want to do, and hopefully you will become successful at doing it. Good Worker are rewarded.

CHAPTER FIVE

RECOGNIZING YOUR ABILITIES

Recognize your power. Where it is and where you want it to be. Where it is that scientists get their information from? Why is it that we are able to put a man on the moon? How is it that we could make rockets and make them work the way they do? How is it possible for mankind to go beneath the sea? How are we able to create life? How are we able to stay alive? Why are we where we are? The truth and or the answers are always there, but someone has to do something to find the answers, and that something is to try. The scientists get their information by and from their hard work, by experimenting. We are able to put men on the moon because we have experimented, plus the desire to do so. We are able to make rockets and make the, go where we want them to go by the will power to succeed, and making important decisions. It is possible for Mankind to go beneath the sea for a long time because we have the technology and the know how and the Nation behind the scientists to make this a reality.

We are able to create life by making fast and important decisions and being persistent. We are able to stay alive because we want to, because we like what we do and we get pleasure from doing it. We are where we are because we want to be here. We like it here. We are here because someone long ago had an idea, and from that idea, here we are. Everything started from an idea.

The very worse you can do with your idea is leave it alone or procrastinate it for another day; never procrastinate on your ideas, you may have found out that the less you put things off the better your possibilities are that you will become successful. A lack of procrastination will ensure you with an opportunity to a successful conclusion. Opportunity is a fair chance to seek your wants and desires in this present world. You can become successful in any job you may have, or in any field you may choose; this means that to be successful you really don't have to succeed in your present job or field, but instead you can do other things while still in your present employment. Discover something and you will have a firsthand experience of what being successful is all about. You can look out in the environment and from it you can envision many things to invent, write about, or make better for the usage of by everyone. There are many wonderful, profited, scenic, and enjoyable things for one to thrive in (in) every walk of life; be it in a professional or a military or a civilian way of life. The final note here and the most important, is that if you want to be a successful person, you must have any of these five characteristics (or all five) or go through these steps:

First- You should have the desire to do whatever you really want to do. Second- You should have enough faith in yourself to accomplish that ever you choose to go into. Third- You have to make some big and a fast decisions (sometimes you will enjoy making those decisions, other times you will be agitated by having to make them) nevertheless you will have to make them (hopefully you will have the proper information and make the right choices; if not it will probably cost you dearly.) Fourth- You have to be persistent and hopefully accurate as well. Fifth- You must be enthusiastic about what you are going to do, for a while at least. If you keep these five steps in mind at all times you will certainly attain whatever you want or try to do. Men could create anything he could imagine, or envision. This brings to mind the first time the NASA jumped into space untethered, entirely alone. "And science fiction became Fact." To simply put it "one heck of a big leap. . ." You too can make or take big leaps into anything that you so wish. Fiction today, Fact tomorrow. This also brings to mind a few quotations I was able to put together or read someplace and have stayed in my mind. What is extraordinary, will always capture the public's imagination. Snow is to men . . . What nature is to the environment. . . A man's home is his palace. Be all you can be. The automobile is like having a sweet lady, knowing you can rest in comfort at a moment's notice.

A place of residence is where a human mind is put to its outer limits, and it most productive in society. If you know everything, there(s) nothing you don't know. I'm not so much moved by winning as I am by a new challenge. Life is beautiful, learn to live, and enjoy it. I included these above quotes (some written by this writer, some not) because as I mentioned in the "Foreword" There are still a lot of possibilities to you as a writer, Entrepreneur, Supervisor, or just worker, again: You can think about anything you want to. You can do anything you want to, (if you really want to).

CHAPTER SIX

LEARNING FROM MISTAKES

There is an old proverb that says "People learn from their mistakes." I really don't see how this can be true; from personal experience people don't really learn from their mistakes. (it would wise to make note of those mistakes but people don't want to recall negative events that happened them in the past) if this was true, I could make a hypothesis and say that people will start making all kinds of mistakes, just to learn or profit from the mistakes. (I realize that people sometimes do make mistakes and yes they do learn a lesson from those mistakes, but pending on the particulars on that mistakes, they may or may not be incarcerated for a period of time or given probation with some supervision involved) If this was the case it would be considerably more difficult, but still if you wanted to succeed in life or in a venture you have every chance to make it come true; there is no stopping you but you (yourself). I am sure that there are people that would swear that they have learned from their mistakes (and it can be true enough), but people are always saying and doing things that are hard to believe. Now when I say that you could become or be a very successful person, a lot of people might read it and say, I don't believe that lie. Now a great majority of the people might say that they know that for one to become successful one must be the master for himself/herself. You are right. You have to take charge of your life, you have to forget the rules, and you have to find out just how crazy you really are (crazy in the sense that you don't know how things are going to turn out but you are ready

To undertake. You become a person that organizes, manages, and assumes the risks of a business; trial and error will determine if you will become successful. Crazy in the sense that just how far you would go to do what you want to accomplish. After you have answered your own questions, ask yourself, where will it all lead me to? When you answer this question, then you have a better idea of how crazy you really are. This does not mean that when you have a good idea about something, you should write it down on paper and then ask questions and get all the answers to them right away.

You could write down the questions and try hard to find the answers don't turn back, but instead continue onward to success do you part. Some people could come up with a good idea and not have to write it down, because they have a photogenic mind, (They always remember). But not all seeking a better life are blessed or gifted as the ones I just mentioned. Another factor that gets in people's way is their jobs. A great number of people don't like what they are doing at work. You talk to them and they reflect what they are going through. They complain that they have to stand all day or they have to sit all day, they are tired of pushing papers, and it never stops. In some of the jobs that I have studied and have done, the people are treated as if they didn't have any rights. There are many people who don't think of themselves as having a right on what goes on in their shop. There are people who slide dangerously into their first job, which will determined the future of their work the rest of their lives.

Many people think that when it comes to their work, they don't have many rights. People are require to report to their supervisors at work and that supervisors will issue the work to be done for that day or week and he/she don't want anything to go wrong until the job is completed. If people were created equal, why then should they (we) be treated different? If people were given good jobs and a good paycheck to go with it, this great country would be even greater. Human drive toward fulfillment as soon as their basic survival needs have been satisfied, not before. When ordinary people feel like they are doing something useful, they try harder. They try harder in putting out more production and get the work done as soon as possible; but when hard working people are not appreciated for doing what they do, they don't care what and how they do the work. They might say, oh hell with him/her/ hell with this/ hell with that etc., etc.

When an employer overhears one employee saying to another, this work is not coming out good, and the other employee answers with, I don't care how it comes out as long as I do my production (quotas). In a case like this, the employees are not being treated as humans but as machinery, or some kind of tool or something to complete the job, not as someone with pride and rights and having feelings. For them work has no meaning. Work must be worthy, worthy of one's talent, and abilities, and it should have an interest, or a purpose. I feel that when one finish a day's work without sense of satisfaction, no sense of accomplishment or anything good, one is being had; as you can see on page 4, I have had nine employers since I started working in 1976 until the writing of this book. (1986) at each one of those jobs I had a problem adjusting to either their income structure, the supervisors foremen being to pushy or demanding, and in some cases doing way to much work for the income being paid at the end of each week (in some cases at the end of every two weeks.) Another problem I had was that every time I was able to land a part-time position on the side, my present employer at the would say that I had to pick one job over the other because it was a conflict of interest; I would leave the part-time position and continue the struggle and never forgot what my goals were (are). I thought about moving from Connecticut to other parts of the Country but every time I would think that if I want success I will become successful right in Bristol.

Included in this chapter you will find a copy of Time Zones and Area Codes of the United States; I included this information because it shows all the states and times for that area, maybe it will help you, as it helped me in making my decision final.

Time Zones and Area Codes

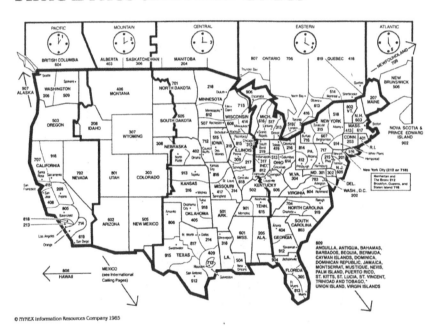

© NYNEX Information Resources Company 1985

CHAPTER SEVEN

READING AND GATHERING INFORMATION

Think big and think Rich. The bigger you think the more desire you will get about doing what you really want to accomplish (overcome). If you want a hundred thousand dollars you will start by imagining just how much money one hundred thousand dollars really is.

You would try to form an image in your mind of stacks of bills, adding up to one hundred thousand dollars. You would start to think how would I get that amount of money? What can I do or sell or create, that would yield me One hundred thousand dollars. Just by thinking in these terms, you will find the answers (or at least, some of the answer). Then you would start to look around you your community to find out, or try to find out ideas that would get you started. You would talk to people and always keep your goals in mind. When you go to the stores, think about what you can make and how you could possibly sell it to the store manager(s). When you are driving around, think about the world you live in, think in terms of; where would this country be without me? (I hope this is not interpreted as a line of conceitedness, it's not intended as such) but instead to illustrate that you really can accomplish any task you participate in; think in terms of what can I do to improve society? Always have in mind the thought that you have a goal to fulfill; and anything (I mean anything) could be it. The best way to find ways to make a lot of money, is by reading books, magazines, or the like, and the cheapest way to go to the library and read books on famous people that made it big. Read as many success books as possible; and don't forget that knowledge is power. The more knowledge you have the stronger you will become intellectualistic. People will listen to what you have to say. You should read as much as possible and after you finish reading a book don't forget to take notes because when you cannot fully remember what the book was about you can refer to your notes; if you don't take notes, it might be wise than to read it a second time. Read books that are factual, read about your town, know what's going on in your own back yard; why? The answer is a simple one; if you know what is going on around you, you have a better chance to succeed than would an outsider (someone from out of town) also, let's say that you worked hard for five or six years, and have saved up one thousand dollars in that period.

Say that a big company is in town looking for a lot big enough to establish its business; but they don't have a place to build it, let's just say that you are well aware of your community and you happen to know of a place where there is a parcel big enough to build such a company; you could either buy it with your one thousand dollars and let the company officials know about the site, or just let them know about the parcel; without buying it, I'm sure they will compensate you for the information. If you are into Real Estate, and you are well informed about the area (geographically) you can buy cheap and sell high. The point is, know your town. Also read a lot about world events. Read books on geography of cities (especially your city), Automotive, psychology, I strongly advice any book on psychology (I have learned a great deal about individuals and people as a whole and even about myself by reading psychology books). If you know what makes people tick, you are in a better position than someone else. You could tell a great about people, just by their body language. Read books on science, you could also learn a lot about science from science books. Read books on how to be a boss, how to be a teacher. How to fix things, how to be a social worker, etc, etc. Read anything that you get your hands on, and if you like technical reading, read on Real Estate, or how to become a Real Estate agent.

Think big and think rich. You can think about yourself as being rich, than act as if you actually are rich, spend your money in a very wise manner. If you think of yourself as being rich, and you act as if you are rich, after a while it would come natural, and you would find ways to better yourself and possibly become rich in the course. The richer you think you ought to be, the harder you will try to become rich. Also you should be in charge at all times; by this I mean, that you don't let anyone run your life. Now I stress this strongly, and that is that you should try to learn as much from other people as possible (just don't be getting in their way, if so they will avoid you and you don't accomplish anything) you can learn a great deal by watching other people conduct their business. If at all possible, spend some time with an attorney, doctor, or anyone in particular that is in a professional field, try to change your vocabulary to match theirs, but don't overdo it; Nothing is duller then to talk to a walking encyclopedia. When you meet someone for the first time don't (I repeat don't) get nervous, breathe deeply and as naturally as possible. Try to interest the person in what you are interested in, be persuasive, but not too much; be kind, but not too much either. Try to get along with everyone, even if you don't like that person. Just because you don't like a person doesn't mean that you cannot do business with them. Be nice to everyone, but not too nice, because people will take advantage of you (if you let them).

If you start on try to start a business, always talk to an attorney. If at all possible try to get the opinion of two different attorneys, and then (only then) draw your own conclusion(s).

Get as much information as possible. Get all the facts before hand if possible. When you try something and fail, don't give up, but do it again, but in a different way. Analyze it step by step, until you find the problem(s) and redness them. Plan your work and work your plan. Another thing is to put your dreams in action. I mentioned earlier to read every book you could get your hands on but I didn't tell you of one that is the best one to read, and that one is the Dictionary. The information in a dictionary is endless. One part that helped me a great deal was the "Famous- Quotation" Section. You can get good ideas from quotations, like: We have nothing to fear except fear itself.

Ambition's like a circle on the water, which never ceases to enlarge itself, till by broad spreading it disperses to nothing. Lend thy serious hearing to what I shall unfold. . .

The two most engaging powers of an author are to make new things familiar, and familiar things new.

Books are a guide in youth, and an entertainment for age. They support us under solitude, and keep us from becoming a burden to ourselves. They help us to forget the crossness of men and things, - compose out our care and our passions, and lay our disappointments asleep. When we are weary of the living, we may repair to the dead, who have nothing of peevishness, pride or design in their conversation. It is a good thing to learn caution by the misfortunes of others. Poor and content is rich enough, but riches, fine less, is as poor as winter, to him that ever fears he shall be poor. Courage consists not in blindly overlooking danger, but in seeing it, and conquering it.

Happy the man, and happy he alone, he, who can call today his own. He who, is secure within, can say tomorrow to thy worst, for I have lived today.

I could continue writing sayings, but I have gotten across my point. You might not see it the way I see it because there are two sides to every story. If you know both sides to each story, where would this world be today? Think about it. For better or for worst. Anyway, what I'm trying to say is that when you try something and it doesn't work out, try it again, but in a different way.

If when you read something and you don't understand it, have someone else read it for you, maybe she/he can read it so it makes sense to you. "If at first you don't succeed, try, try, try, again. So remember, look for the good things in life, in yourself and in others. Be true to yourself, and help others to understand.

CHAPTER EIGHT

ANALYZING YOUR ABILITIES

Analyze your abilities, etc. By this I mean that most people might sit down and start to think of what they did wrong last month, last week, and in the past few hours ago. Now this is not such a bad idea, but some people think too much about the bad things that they did, and not enough about the good things that they should do or be doing. There are a lot of new things out there to be accomplish by all of us. Some business men don't go to their utmost potential because they are afraid that they might fail. If you don't try something because you are afraid that you might fail you are not trying to succeed because you are leaving yourself short.

Now if you were afraid and still went ahead and tried, who knows what profits might be realized by you, just by trying to do better, or what career might open up for you, all for following through with your idea(s). You should work on your strengths and not so much on your weakness. Too many people append too much time finding or trying to find their weak spots, and none (or very little) on their strengths. They should see it as "Well I can do this thing very good, and that thing there I cannot do so good, so I will concentrate on that one". Now some people should try to work on what they do best, and a little on the next thing that they do fairly good, and so on. Just don't spend too much time on any one subject (venture), unless you too have a long time to do it in. A very important thing that everyone needs, is self-trust in order to succeed. After you have self-trust, than is when you should go into action; by this I mean that if you don't trust yourself to start a venture a finish it (or take it as far as possible) you should not attempt to take on the responsibility or that venture, but if you have faith in yourself, if you have the energy and have found answers to your questions, than you are ready for action. By action I mean, trying out your ideas to see what success rate you will have, or where it will lead you. Ask yourself, where am I now (today), and where will this take me? What is my next step? Of course like I mentioned above, if you have found answers to your questions, then action should be your next step. The individual who goes at something as if they know what they are doing (with answers to their questions), they will get more pleasure out of it. If every time you want to accomplish (start a venture) something; you start to think (negative) like: oh what if something bad happens? Or what if I fall short of my goals? I hope that you don't let this kind of thinking overcome you, but instead you should overcome it. To fulfill is to conquer, to conquer is to succeed. I am not saying that you should not think of what might happen on the negative side, but what I'm saying is, don't let it overcome you. Don't let it get you down, as a good idea you might want to follow a guideline for designing your own investments/ventures. You should make your own decisions, and if you have to change it, do so gradually, but stick to it like glue; remember this idea could bring you a fortune, or everything that you ever wanted, and possibly more. So make your decisions fast, and don't change them. If you make a fast decision and it turns out for the worst, remember that in every crisis there is an opportunity. There is something good in every bad experience.

This book was not written to scare you, but to try to give you some confidence so that if you want to try writing or something, you should try it regardless of the consequences. If you want to make lots of money, you have to make fast decisions, and again, regardless of consequences. Most of the business man I have spoken to tell me that the way to make money, is by following through with their first ideas. For example: if they come up with an idea that would bring them some income, they in most cases, would gamble on it. If it works out, they gain a great deal, but if it doesn't well then they loose, but many times when they win they really win. This is what you have to practice and follow. Why shouldn't you be able to have everything you want or wish to accomplish?

Success does not happen automatically, you have to make it happen; you have to try different methods, until you find all the right answers, than you can acquire that which you envisioned. Here again, as I have said in chapters before; if you really want something you can just go out and find a way to get it, there might be some work, if not a lot of hard work, but if you really want it, you will succeed in whatever task you involve yourself in. some people after they read or hear me speak, tell me that one cannot have, or get everything that one wants. My answer is; you can always certainly try. There are people that never accomplish anything or get what they want because they just don't try hard enough. I am sure that if you really want something bad enough, you will get it, or come very close to getting it.

I read a book not long ago that stated, you should put a price on everything you want, this way, if you are willing to pay the price, no matter what it is, then you will get possession of it, one way or the other. The value of what you want is expressed in the price than you are willing to pay for it. You also have to become more careful in the handling of your money. Some people go out and don't know how to spend their money. They might see something appealing and use their credit cards, and when the bill arrives; they cannot even remember what it was they bought. Nowadays you have to keep an eye on your money, otherwise it will vanish very quickly. If and when you go out shopping, don't look something over, but study it and make an option and after you make that opinion, then if it passes, buy it. Buy things that will last for at least two years, or that would stay in style for a while after a buy it. All these factors contributes to your success; remember, the key factor is their willingness to change. If you want to change, the world is yours. I myself have changed in many ways and yet there is more change to come. I know that if I meet it half way I can benefit from every one of those changes; and like I mentioned before you can also benefit from every one of those changes; and like I mentioned before you can also benefit from a crisis (even though this is not to say that every time you change, it will be bad or that it will become a crisis to endure). It's really up to you and your ideality(ies).

CHAPTER NINE

DOING OR MAKING SOMETHING

Don't just sit there, do something! Make something worthwhile. Invent something. You should try to do something in which you never have done before, or something you have confidence in. people make or invent things for a number of reasons. Many invent for rewards that it brings with it, not really knowing what; others invent for the recognition; yet others invent for the satisfaction of having accomplish something worthwhile. You should try to invent something for the use and pleasure of doing it, for pure satisfaction. From there you will get pleasure, an income, and recognition, and maybe more. Do you know how it is to do something and every time people see you, congratulate you, for doing what you did? It's a great feeling; even though after a while it will annoy you, due the fact that you will hear it so often that you might not belief what people are saying; but then you get down to thinking on how you thought and felt the day after you did it- (whatever it was you did) and will feel the same way once again, it would be like doing it for the first time. Then you would do something else and go through the same cycle all over again; and so on. You could work on this. You start to feel like you don't trust people, when you feel like this, you should think or try to think in positiveness. I think that since you have gotten this far on this book, you should make some practical resolutions for upgrading yourself this and every year from now on.

You will be surprise at how fast you can change for the better. Don't be afraid to do something that you have never done before. Ask yourself, what could possibly happen if I do something that I am afraid of doing?

If you don't do it, then how would you know that it's going to fail? But if you try it, it could surprise you on how easy it really was. Now I'm not saying that you should go out and do something which might either cause you harm or get you into trouble; but what I'm saying is try it a ways and if you see its not beneficial, then stop and try it another way. Also, know what you are doing. Don't try to do something blindly, but instead think about how you will attempt to overcome the obstacles that may get in your way. At times you can think about something mentally and you work at it to perfection in your mind, but when the time comes to actually practice it, you either forget it, or do it in a different way, so it's very important to write it down and do it exactly how its written. Another point that I want to get across. Don't be like a lot of people I know, they are always so busy enjoying themselves that they have very little time to think on the great and many opportunities that life has to offer them. The only way that you can gain success is by trying to accomplish what appears to be impossible. The more impossible it looks, the harder you should try to accomplish or overcome it, until you do conquer it, then you could set another goal to conquer and don't stop or even slowdown until you have overcome it as well. One thing that I must caution you on, "Your family and friends". They might be trying to help you according to their lifestyle, and experiences, but most of the time they will tell you not to do something they paid a price for and if you listen to them, you too

might pay the same price, and the problem will not get solve. They might say that you should not try to attempt it, here is where and when you should try the hardest to excel and to succeed, by applying all your concentration and efforts to the success of this venture (problem). When you try something for the first time you should be very cautious, alert, and above all sharp and wise, be ready to try as many different ways as humanly possible, and if still out of reach, don't give up, but put it aside and get the real answers before you started again (don't forget it though). If at first you don't succeed, try, try, and try, again. And for those that want to start their own business, because it could prove to be very costly or a bad idea. Know every single detail about your business, the more you know about a business, or a subject the easier it is to talk or understand it. Know where everything is and check on the facts on a daily basis (know the facts very closely and very well). If you think that something is just not right, take the time and check it, move it, or rearrange it to your liking. You should be or do what you think is best for you and your venture and or business. Be alert so you don't get hurt. I read a book that said if you look within your own mind, you can find any answer that you are looking for. The answers are there, all you have to do is find them and use them as best as you know how. Find where the problems are, look them over, and come up with a solution, either in favor of or against it. There is nothing that you cannot think about, and if you think about any particular subject, or matter you will start getting answers you are looking for.

The mind is like a machine, it can take a subject and know everything about it, it reflects back everything from the time of birth, to the time of (near) death, or until death and beyond (my opinion is that when one is about to die one can know and must be ready for it. The mind is a most powerful instrument with its own secrets and it can even play tricks on us. It can make you remember as well as forget things, but with practice you can conquer it too. The mind has numerous connections to different parts of the body.

Mind- The unconscious and conscious processes that perceive, conceive, comprehend, evaluate, and reason; the mind can be consider a mechanical device that serves to perform functions of the human brain for command, guidance, or computation; so if you want to know about anything of interest pertaining to humans or any other subject the mind can supply you with all the answers, even if you have to spend time looking for those answers (sometimes looking for an answer can take a while to realize) and when you find it, you will realize how easy it really was, so take on the challenge and conquer it as best as you can. Every time you do something, do it with complete confidence and absolutely no negative thoughts whatsoever. . Make your choices as if you are one hundred percent sure, and when you make a direct move towards a goal it will be returned tenfold. Do what you feel you have to do, without any regrets. If you do a good job, it is because you did some research, and now you feel you can continue the process, on a successful note. One example that comes to mind is that if you are happy and treated as a human being and a friend you not only do a good job but you as a worker (writer, whatever you are into) would like the work more and will try to perform at a higher level. Remember that: A happy employee is a happy employer. I think that if supervisors speak to their employees and speak to them at a level where they can understand what is being said everything would not be as bad as it is (at least when I worked in a shop). There is nothing solid or not that you cannot conquer. Always be your own person. Be yourself, this way you avoid giving the impression that you are one way and actually being someone else. Do what you think and feel is right, but first think about it extensively. Again: Be alert, so you don't get hurt.

CHAPTER TEN

WHAT ARE YOU CREATING AND WHO ARE YOU CREATING FOR

What are you creating and who are you creating for? You should create not for income, but for an easier way of life. When you dedicate yourself to the betterment of society, you have everything on your favor. First of all, you have the public (if you have or make something that would interest or benefit them). That's millions of people, imagine how much that can produce in monetary terms; but again don't invent or create something for the money, but instead for an easier way of life for mankind as a whole. You don't have to invent anything to make money, you can establish a product, or can write articles, you can write a novel, you can help people do things, but here too people would say that is a creation, and in a way it is. A way to invent something is to think about a specific object for a few days and then purposely put it aside or forget about it, or continue to make changes until the product becomes what you feel is completed.

I read a book some time ago that said: if you think about something and really cannot find the answers to complete the product maybe it's because you are forcing yourself, and things would only get worse when force is used or applied. When an idea is no longer in your mind and it was, try to not think about it until the mind brings it back to recollection, first the thought, then the answer. I don't know just how true this is, but why not try it. Maybe you can discover or invent (create) something from the experiment(s), or it might work the way it supposed to for you. This is what I mean, when I say that you can do anything.

You could think of any subject or anything which to you sounds like someone must have invented or created and is selling well, but maybe you are the creator (if you go ahead a complete it, you can be the first one to have made it). You, right now could maybe think of or do something that can yield a great deal of a fame, stature, recognition, and of course finances, so don't let anyone get in your way to success. Try everything very carefully, because that might be the one to put you in the road to success (fame, or make you very rich), so start right now, do a lot of reading and a great deal of studying, it could only pay off in the long run. When you start to read or to try to find the answers to something, make sure that no one interrupts you because it could cause your project to fall short or even fail. It would be very wise and advisable to put a desk or a table and a chair in a room or anywhere you can go to think by yourself. When you study or write, are you under pressure? Some people are very creative under a lot of pressure; but others would fall apart. You have to be in the middle, or practice working under pressure. If you are always under pressure at work, or at home, let the person(s) that you feel that they are pressuring you without due cause. Let them know that if you were not under pressure so much, you could be more productive and useful. Life is too wonderful to be lived under pressure. If you could have fun while working, everything would be all right. The so call "fun" you can have at work is a very limited one, even though you can enjoy yourself at times while working. You can be sociable at work, but don't overdo it, you could work hard but again don't overdo it either, unless you feel that if you do, it will be recognize by management or your supervisor and there being a possibility for advancement in salary or a better job, than you can work faster than everyone else and make sure that the boss knows that you are working harder and faster than everyone else. If you work more than everyone and then you have to speak to someone when you are not supposed to the supervisor(s) won't tell you to get to work, or something like that. Anyway back to the title: What are you creating and who are you creating for?

One thing that I want to say, and that is that when you have an idea or a hunch, go for it; but again don't force yourself if you cannot come up with a solution fast enough. If you force yourself you won't get anything done or get anywhere. If you go at it in an easy manner, you just might find the answers you're looking for. Another thing that I want to get across, is that you might have the greatest idea that you think will yield a great deal of money, and fame as well, but because of your age, maybe no one will listen to you or what you have to say. That's why in the previous chapters, I said that your vocabulary should match that of who you are talking to. If you want them to listen to what you want to say, at times you might say, I wish I was ten years older, and had more experience. Well if you continue thinking like this and do a lot of reading as well as a lot of research, maybe in ten years you will be just like you thought ten years before; Just don't ever stop or even think about slowing down. When you feel like you cannot take anymore, if you overcome this feeling then you will be one step closer to your goal. There are so many steps before you reach your goal. So read a lot and do a great deal of thinking. You can turn yourself into an expert. "How"? By reading, researching, and schooling (practicing) what you read, and by being alert. "Be alert, don't get hurt". The best time to do all the above things are when you just graduated from High School, or college, or any university, because the ideas will be still fresh in your mind. You know, a lot of High School students have a lot of good ideas, but they don't know how to develop them or take them steps further, so do the College graduates, and the drop outs as well. I think that you already know that though. So I won't get in to that anymore. A very strange way to come up with ideas are to stare into space and think. I said that it was strange. (This statement is very much true, at least it is to me. If you just stare at or into space, you are letting your mind wonder into places which you don't ordinary think about, and since you don't think about it often, when you do, you might hit upon a great idea.

Like I stated in previous chapters, when you have an idea, go for it, and do your very best and it will get you somewhere. (I find myself writing this statement over and over), but that's because it really works. If you go after an idea at the right price, and for the right reasons, you have it made. You might say, what can I do? Well here is a very big and wide field. You can make a better mouse trap, you can perfect something in existence, or since you have an idea of how many things are in existence I won't get into naming them here. Just try to invent or create something, you will be surprised at the things that you can do.

Remember, if you want to be successful always have in mind your goals, and have an open mind about anything and everything around you. That which is around you is a great place to start to look for better ways to improve society. You are the one who can make the difference.

CHAPTER ELEVEN

CONTROLLING YOUR MIND

Think Positive on a constant cycle learning basis on a daily manner. There are a great number of people who think a great deal, but about the wrong things. They spend a lot of time thinking about if they should move toward their goals. Their move might fail and their friends might embarrass them. Think nothing of it. If you feel like trying something and thing that your friends might ridicule you, do it anyway. If you spend too much time thinking whether you should do it and be ridiculed, or leave it alone, you are wasting your valuable time. If you do it and it turns out alright, than I am sure that your friends will be interested the next time, so don't let ridicules get you down because, if you do you are the one that will lose, no one else. There might be some "so called" Friends that since they cannot do it, (don't know how to do it, or is scared to death to try it), or just don't want to do it, so they ridicule you when they discover that you are going to try it, or you tell them that you will try it with enthusiasm. They do this so you won't try it or so you won't try it or so you won't succeed in life. If your eye is on success follow your thoughts. If your eye is on making money, than you should find out how it feels when money ways there are to making real money. At times (or should I say) most of the times you need money to make money. This in some cases is true, but I'm sure that you (we) can device a plane to overcome just that. Now, ask yourself, how do I get some of this money so I could use it to make more money? I tend to answer it very easily.

First, you can run errands to a second party in return for a commission or something that has a value, which can be exchange for money or whatever you wish; You can write a book on a number of subjects already about you; or you could show people how to do things, (how to be a better cook, how to catch a fish, how to and the best places to hunt, how to peel potatoes, or even, how to lose all your money in the market or on drugs), or you can even make something. You can become a Real Estate agent, and take it from there. All you have to do is get yourself enthused enough to actually try something for the first time and try to succeed in it. If you really feel like doing something to satisfy the public and in turn your ego as well, believe me, you not only can but you will.

If you have enough will power to do it, you can and will. If you have the mind to study something until you fully understand or become an expert, you will do anything in which you set your mind on doing. Believe it or not you can. If you want to change, you really can. If you are determined to change something for the better you can too. Just say to yourself as often as possible that you want to be successful. If you say it often enough you will subconsciously convince your conscience, than your conscience will convince your body which in turn will get the job done. Than you can take it from there to continue on that road to success. Some people after they have gone through all of the above steps, and it's all up to them to continue, give up or start to back off, or slow down. When you have gone through all of the above steps, you are home free; by this I mean that after you go through the steps, anything if not everything that you do from then on will result in success or very close to it. Here you have convinced yourself that you can do anything, as long as you want to really do it, and are willing to perhaps pay the consequences. If you are willing to take some risks, then you most likely will benefit more than anything else. But if you want to play and not pay, well then hang it up right now and here! Because you won't get very far. You have to be able to say, I'm going to do this thing and look for the answers because it's there all you have to do is find it and use it to your advantage. There is another thing I want to get across. Controlling your mind. That's right. I read a book once that said, if you can control your mind, you control your destiny. I am a strong believer in this statement, because that is what this book is all about. If your mind wants something and you stand firm and resist, you in a way have controlled your mind, even when the uneasy feelings are brought within the mind itself. It is this very same control in which I am saying you should try to get or be part of. If you come across it, hold it because it will bring you anything that you always wanted. Now if you have this attitude, this by no means that you are perfect, far from it. What this does is make you become aware of what you are doing, and what to watch out for, also a positive feeling towards accomplishing that which you are striving for. If you make a mistake along the way, you should be ready to encounter it, and deal with it as best as you can, as long as you don't let that mistakes get you down, you will rebound and start again. The only person that does not make any mistakes, is he/she that never does anything, for fear of not succeeding in that task, (even though he/she is always talking about his fellow human and not doing anything to improve himself.) If you ever come across a person like this one above, it would be a very wise idea to stay away from him/her, so he/she won't give you negative thoughts, or feelings about your fellow man in which your views are different. You have to like, and try to make friends with everyone, regardless of race, color, or creed. You have to make people like and want to be with you. You have to make people believe in you and what you say too, and one way to accomplish this is by telling it as it is. This way they believe in you and what you say, in turn you believe in them, and what they say. It's as simple as that. You also have to be good to yourself. Make people know you as you want them to know you. In some cases you have to use your imagination and not do anything until the time is just right. Don't speak until you are asked a question. Don't confront a challenge if you have not gotten ready for it, because I most cases you will lose the fight for that very important struggle. So confront the challenge, find ways to conquer it, than conquer it. Try to know everything about it and then, (and only then) try to solve it. So if you want to try something and if I was a professional, and you asked me for my opinion, I would say, try it regardless of the consequences, if there are any involve. But it is a good idea to go into something thinking and planning to find something wrong with it and be prepare to deal with it. "Be alert, so you don't get hurt. Now as an expert have to make new friends and respect what they have to say, even if you don't agree with what they think or say. Speaking of success, the very successful person is always willing to listen to new ideas from their friends, even if you think that they are not considered ideas at your level (whether plus or minus). To be successful, one must search for success regardless of the consequences. If one goes after success, not worrying to much about the consequences, but firmly thinking that one will succeed, one can do nothing but succeed. If one looks for success, success will find one also. So alert looking. One can conquer their fantasy(ies). If one feels and thinks that one day he/she will become a millionaire, one will indeed become rich, or extremely wealthy, but you have to try, research, study, look, speak with the right people, and then go into it as if there is no tomorrow. You should at times think like the world not function without you. That's not being conceited, but from it you will get a tremendous confidence building that you desperately need on a constant cycle. The confidence that you get from thinking in this way would impair any negative thoughts that still remain in your mind. It would boast you up one hundred percent, and the feeling would be a great one, and so great that you will do anything in which you set out to accomplish. One must feel like the King of the mountain. One must also do as they feel or wish, to become a success. You would also have to overcome your fears. If you conquer fear, you have nothing to fear, and everything to conquer. So do what you have to do, and do it to the best of your ability. The success of most things depend.

CHAPTER TWELVE

THE LAST THING TO DO

The last thing to do, after you have thought about what you want to do, and after you have written it down on paper, so you won't forget it, also after you have red and talked to people about what you want to accomplish, or what you want to become. From here on, if you are still determined to accomplish, or become what you thought you have to, just do what you think is right. Think on what you are doing on a constant continuous basis, never forgetting your original goals and what must be done to reach a successful conclusion. You have to think about it a lot, and when you communicate your views to someone else, speak as clear as you possibly can, so whomever you are speaking to would understand what you are saying on a clear note, talk slow if need be and with determination; Remember, you have done a lot of research, so you consider yourself an expert, and it would be nice if you could look or talk like one. You have to do things even though they might scare you somewhat, but it would have to be done. There is one thing that I feel should not be communicate (at least not until you have accomplished your immediate goals) that is "Your Business practice (habits) and dealings", this should be kept confidential so you can enjoy success, profits, and happiness, and above all, Superiority over the mediocre individual (who if he/she knew your plan for success would undoubtingly pass it along to his/her friend, and his friend will pass it to his friend, so on and so forth; after all, here is where your experience will come from. To be successful, you upon knowing how long it will take to succeed, and not slowing down until your ideas are fulfill. Success could be acquire in many ways, one of which is by traveling. When one travel to places where he/she never has been to, they get new ideas and a different feelings about the surroundings. I like to go hiking for many reasons; one because it gives me the exercise that I need; second because it clears up my mind about daily problems and world events, it makes me think in terms of reaching the top and having fun while climbing up. Third, because once you are at the top, you can look down and see what you went through, you can think about it in a slower pace but remembering every move that you made going up. If you were to apply this same method in your everyday business activity you would probably be in a better position than you are now. When you think about a goal and go after it and accomplish it you can reflect back and see the moves and choices you had to make. You would benefit a great deal from reflecting back on how you got over the obstacles, you can also use those same thought patterns to accomplish other goals. You can continue the same principals until you get to where you want to go or be at. In previous chapters I talked about the mind and how great it was (is); now I want to add to it a bit. The mind is the most powerful machine in the world. That's right. If you were put in an isolated room at birth and left along, you won't learn anything because you would not need to feel wanted; but if you were put in that same isolated room with a group you sooner or later would probably want to lead the others, thus finding ways to make them listen and believe in what you are doing or saying. There is no present problem with this until someone else starts to want to feel like he/she can make the differences or want to feel wanted, thus wanting change, with or without the help of others. If you want to accomplish something but don't know how or where to go for information, just go out and have a good time, but with the thought in mind that you are looking for an answer to this specific task (subject) matter. Go jogging, or for a long walk (maybe someone will offer you a ride and the answer that you are looking for); go swimming, go play baseball or basketball, the thing to do is do something, anything. Anything in which you can profit from and in a legal way. If not mentally, then by all means physically, and keeping both "Drug Free".

Be number one in something. You could be the best in playing Chess, or the best in baseball, or the best and most charming person in your city (meaning that a lot of people should and must know who you are). You can be the best at writing articles, or you can be the first to write a book all in numbers. Yes in numbers. I would like to also write you about Drugs, I really think that people who do drugs, not in words but in numbers, to give you an idea how this can be accomplished.

A B C D E F G H I J K L M N O P Q R S T U V W X Y Z

1 2 3 4 5 6 7 8 9 10 11 12 13 14 15 16 17 18 19 20 21 22 23 24 25 26

4-I8-2I-7-I9

I-I4-25 9-I4-7-I8-5-4-9-5-I4-20 2I-I9-5-4 9-I4 3-8-5-I3-9-I9-20-I8-25,
I6-8-I-I8-I3-I-3-25, 4-25-5-9-I4-7, I5-I8 20-8-5 I2-9-II-5; I-I4-25
I3-5-4-9-3-9-I4-I-I2 I9-2I-2-I9-20-I-I4-3-5 6-I5-I8 9-I4-20-5-I8-
I4-I-I2 I5-I8 5-24-20-5-I8-I4-I-I2 2I-I9-5; I5-6-20-5-I4, 8-I-2-9-20
6-I5-I8-I3-9-I4-7 I3-5-4-9-3-93I4-I-I2 I9-2I-2-I9-20-I-I4-3-5; I4-I-
I8-3-I5-20-9-3; 3-I5-I3-I3-I5-4-9-20-25 20-8-I-20 9-I9 I5-22-5-I8-
I-2-2I-I4-4-I-I4-20, I5-I8 9-I4 5-24-3-5-I9-I9 I5-6 4-5-I3-I-I4-4 9-I4
20-8-5 I3-I-I8-II-5-20. I4-I-I8-3-I5-20-9-3 I5-I8 I6-I5-9-I9-I5-I4-I5-
2I-I9 I9-2I-2-I9-20-I-I4-3-5; I-I4-25 I9-2I-2-I9-I5-I4-I5-2I-I9 I9-2I-
2-I9-20-I-I4-3-5; I-I4-25 I9-2I-2-I9-20-I-I4-3-5 2I-I9-5-4 9-I4 20-I8-
5-I-20-9-I4-7 4-9-I9-5-I-I9-5 I5-I9 I8-5-I2-9-5-22-9-I4-7 I6-I-9-I4.

23-8-5-I4 25-I5-2I 9-I4-20-I8-I5-I4-2I-3-5 25-I5-2I-I8 I3-9-I4-4
I-I4-4 2-I5-4-25 20-I5 2I-I4-I6-I8-5-I8-3-I8-9-2-5-4 4-I8-2I-7-I9,
25-I5-2I I-I8-5 9-I4-I0-2I-I8-9-I4-7 2-I5-20-8-9-I4-7 25-I5-2I-I8-I9-
5-I2-6 I-I4-4 20-8-I5-I9-5 I-I4-20-I5-24-9-3-I-20-5-4. 20-8-5 I2-
I5-I4-7 I-23-I-9-20-5-4 3-2I-I8-5-? 20-I5 23-8-I5? 20-I5 I9-I5-I3-5
I6-5-I5-I6-I2-5, I4-I5 I3-I-20-20-5-I8 8-I5-23 I9-I3-I-I2-I2 4-I5-
I9-I-7-5 20-8-5-25 20-I-II-5, 9-20 23-9-I2-I2 I-6-6-5-3-20 2-I5-20-8
I3-9-I4-4 I-I4-4 2-I5-4-25 20-I5 I-I4 2I-I4-3-I5-I4-20-I8-I5-I2-I2-
I-2-I2-5 2I-I4-I6-I8-5-4-9-3-20-I-2-I2-5 I9-9-4-5 I-6-6-5-3-20 (I9),
I-I4-4 9-20-I9 I9-20-9-I2-I2 I-I4 9-I2-I2-5-7-I-I2 I4-5-7-I-20-9-22-5
23-I-25 20-I5 4-5-I9-20-I8-I5-25 25-I5-2I-I8 8-5-I-I2-20-8.

9-6 9-20-I9 I4-I5-20 I6-I8-5-I9-3-I8-9-2-5-4 20-I5 25-I5-2I 6-I5-I8 I9-
I5-I3-5-20-8-9-I4-7 I3-5-4-9-3-I-I2-I2-25, 25-I5-2I I9-8-I5-2I-I2-4
I4-I5-20 4-I5 I-I4-25 20-25-I6-5 I5-6 4-I8-2I-7-I9. 6-I8-9-5-I4-4

I3-9-7-8-20 2-5 I9-5-I2-I2-9-I4-7 25-I5-2I 4-I8-2I-7-I9 (9-6 8-5/I9-
8-5 9-I9 I8-5-I-I2-I2-25 6-I8-9-5-I4-4) 8-5/I9-8-5 23-9-I2-I2 7-5-
20 25-I5-2I 20-8-5 I8-5-I-I2 20-8-9-I4-7; (23-8-9-3-8 9-I9 2-I-4
5-I4-I5-2I-7-8); 9-6 8-5/I9-8-5, I0-2I-I9-20 3-I-I2-I2-I9 8-9-I3/8-5-
I8-I9-5-I2-6 6-I8-9-5-I4-4 25-I5-2I I8-5-I-I2-I2-25 4-I5-I4. '20 II-
I4-I5-23 23-8-I-20 9-I4 20-8-5 23-I5-I8-I2-4 20-8-5-25 I-I8-5 I9-
5-I2-I2-9-I4-7 25-I5-2I. I9-I5-I3-5 I6-5-I5-I6-I2-5 23-9-I2-I2 4-I5
I-I2-I3-I5-I9-20 I-I4-25-20-8-9-I4-7 6-I5-I8 I3-I5-I4-5-25 I-I4-4 I9-
5-I2-I2-9-I4-7 9-I2-I2-5-7-I-I2 4-I8-2I-7-I9 2I-I9-2I-I-I2-I2-25 20-
8-5 6-9-5-I2-4= 20-8-I-20-I9 I5-I4-5 6-9-5-I2-4 20-8-I-20 25-I5-2I
I9-8-I5-2I-I2-4 I9-20-I-25 I-23-I-25 6-I8-I5-I3. 8-5/I9-8-5 23-8-I5
4-I5-5-I9 4-I8-2I-7-I9, I9-8-I5-2I-I2-4 2-5 I-2-I2-5 I-I4-4 3-I-I6-I-
2-I2-5 20-I5 I6-I-25 20-8-5 I6-I8-9-3-5, I4-I5-20 I5-I4-I2-25 6-I5-I8
20-8-5 9-I2-I2-5-7-I-I2 4-I8-2I-7 2-2I-20 9-6 25-I5-2I 7-5-20 3-I-2I-
7-8-20 23-9-20-8 9-20, I6-I2-2I-I9 I-I2-I2 20-8-5 I4-5-7-I-20-9-22-5
I-6-6-5-3-20-I9 20-8-I-20 9-20 23-9-I2-I2 2-I8-9-I4-7 25-I5-2I-I8
2-I5-4-9-I2-25 6-2I-I4-3-20-9-I5-I4-I9. 2-5 3-I-I8-5-6-2I-I2 I-I4-4
"2-5 I-I2-5-I8-20, I9-I5 25-I5-2I 4-I5-I4-'20 7-5-20 8-2I-I8-20."

9-6 I9-I5-I3-5 I5-I4-5 I5-I4-4-5 I5-6-6-5-I8 25-I5-2I 4-I8-2I-7-I9, I0-2I-I9-20
I9-I-25 I4-I5!

"2-5 6 -I8-5-5 I-I4-4 5-I4-I0-I5-25 20-8-I-20 23-8-9-3-8 I-I3-5-I8-9-
3-I 8-I-I9 20-I5 I5-6-6-5-I8."

				Common Drugs		
Name	Chemical or Trade Names: Slang	Source	Classification	Medical Use	Effects Sought	Long-Term or Heavy-Use Symptoms
Heroine	Diacetyl morphine; Horse, Junk, Smack, Scag, Stuff	Semisynthetic (from morphine)	Narcotic	Pain relief	Euphoria Prevent withdrawal discomfort	Addiction* Constipation: Loss of appetite Toxic syndrome
Morphine	Morphine Sulphate; White Stuff, M.	Natural (from opium)	Narcotic	Pain relief	Euphoria Prevent withdrawal discomfort	Addiction* Constipation: Loss of appetite Toxic syndrome
Cocaine	Coke; Snow, Flake, Toot, Star dust, Happy dust, Bernie	Natural (from coca, not cocoa)	Stimulant Local anesthetic	Local anesthesia	Excitation, Talkativeness	Depression* Convulsions
Marijuana Hashish	Cannabis Sativa; Pot, Grass, Tea, Dagga, Kif, Joint, Reefer, Weed, Dope	Natural (from hemp)	Relaxant Euphoriant in high doses hallucinogen	Experimental Study	Relaxation increase euphoria or perceptions	Possible psychological addiction* Possible lung, memory , perception or sexual damage
LSD	Lysergic acid diethylamide; Acid; Sugar, Cubes, Trips, Windowpane, Blotter	Semisynthetic (from ergot alkaloids)	Hallucinogen	Experimental study	Insightful experiences* Exhilaration Distortion of senses	May intensify existing psychosis, *panic reactions
Nicotine	Nicotinia tabacum; Fag, Coffin nail	Natural (from tobacco)	Stimulant- Sedative	Sedative Emetic	Calmness Sociability	Emphysema, lung, mouth and throat cancer* Cardiovascular damage* Loss of appetite * Addiction
Codeline	Methylmorphine; Schoolboy	Natural (from opium) Semi synthetic (from morphine	Narcotic	Ease pain and coughing	Euphoria Prevent withdrawal discomfort	Addiction* Constipation Loss of appetite Toxic syndrome
Methadone	Dolophine amidone; Dolly	Synthetic	Narcotic	Pain relief	Prevent withdrawal discomfort	Addiction* Constipation Loss of appetite Toxic syndrome

				Common Drugs		
Name	Chemical or Trade Names: Slang	Source	Classification	Medical Use	Effects Sought	Long-Term or Heavy-Use Symptoms
Mescaline	Buttons, Beans, Cactus	Natural (from peyote)	Hallucinogen	None	Insightful experiences* Exhilaration Distortion of senses	May intensify existing psychological problems
Quaaludes	Methaqualone; Ludes, Soaps, Quacks	Synthetic	Sedative hypnotic	Sedation	Anxiety reduction	Addiction with severe withdrawal symptoms Possible convulsions Toxic syndrome
Barbiturates	Phenobarbital, Nembutal, Seconal, Amytal, Blue devils, Yellow jackets, Blue heavens, Downers, Barbs	Synthetic	Sedative hypnotic	Sedation, Relieve high blood pressure, epilepsy, hyperthyroidism	Anxiety reduction, Euphoria	Addiction with severe withdrawal symptoms Possible convulsions Toxic syndrome
Aspirin	Acetylsalicylic acid	Synthetic	Analgesic	Pain relief, Fever reduction	Pain relief	Possible gastrointestinal irritation or bleeding Possible toxic syndrome
Aspirin Substitutes	Acetaminophen; Tylenol, Datril, Excedrin and numerous drug combinations	Synthetic	Analgesic	Pain relief, Fever reduction	Pain discomfort relief	May produce toxic syndrome such as stupor, convulsions, anemia or abnormal bleeding
Psilocybin	Magic mushrooms:, Mushroom, Losninos	Natural (from psilocybe)	Hallucinogen	None	Insightful experiences Exhilaration Distortion of senses	May intensify existing psychological problems

				Common Drugs		
Name	Chemical or Trade Names: Slang	Source	Classification	Medical Use	Effects Sought	Long-Term or Heavy-Use Symptoms
PCP	Phencyclidin; Angel dust, Hog, Horse tranquilizer, Crystal	Synthetic	Effects unpredictable, can vary with dose Stimulant* Analgesic, Anesthetic and Hallucinogen	Experimental study* Veterinary anesthetic	Omnipotence Sense alteration	Flashbacks- Prolonged anxiety *Social withdrawal* Toxic syndrome *Full range unknown
Amphetamines	Benzedrine, Dexedrine, Methedrine, Speed, Bennies, Peppills, Hearts, Wakeups, Uppers	Synthetic	Sympathomimetic	Relieve mild depression, Control appetite, and narcolepsy	Alertness Activeness	Loss of appetite Delusions* Hallucinations and Toxic psychosis
Alcohol	Ethanol, Ethyl alcohol, Booze, Juice	Natural (from grapes, fruits, fermentation etc	Sedative hypnotic	Solvent Antiseptic Dietary	Sense alteration* Anxiety reduction* Sociability	Cirrhosis* Toxic Psychosis* Neurologic damage* Addiction
Tranquilizers	Valium, Librium, Miltown, Equanil	Synthetic	Sedative relaxant	Sedative	Relaxation Calmness	Possible addiction with severe withdrawal symptoms *Toxic syndrome
Caffeine	Coffee, Cafenoir, Alkaloid	Natural (from coffee, beans, tea, Kola nuts and cocoa-beans; Used in many soft drinks	Stimulant	Stimulant	Alertness Sociability	Jitteriness and mild addiction
Inhalants		Variety of household and industrial chemicals	Varied: Stimulant Sedative, Hallucinogen		Euphoria Distortion of senses;	Toxic syndromes: brain, Kidney, liver, sexual and other tissue damage

ABOUT THE AUTHOR

Born in Puerto Rico: 1959
Moved to New York City: Bronx and other areas
Special Curriculum.
Moved to Springfield, Massachusetts
Main stream Curriculum: Sojourn
Moved to Bristol, Connecticut: Sixth grade on.
Education: Grade 1-3 Ok: New York
Repeated 3rd grade, then Jumped to 6th grade.
Memorial Boulevard School = Middle School: Graduated.

Bristol Central High School = Graduated = 1988.
C.P.I. Computer Processing Institute = Graduated = 1991.
Saint Joseph College: Gengras Center: High School unit: 1992
"Teacher Assistant.

Employment: High School Job: Stop and Shop (15hrs. w/k.)
Local Job Market: here and there, did this and that, but no career.

Had Dreams, Desires, and Aspirations,
Little know how, and or education.

Read Books to escape, travel, and know stuff.
Reading let me to writing and knowing what to read,
And where to get knowledge.

Setting a goal, and going after it, working on it, and becoming successful at the conclusion.
If at first, you don't succeed,
Try- try- try again
Never give into defeat:
Peace and Prosper.

Recreation: I enjoy power walking, mountain Bicycling, Skating (on-line), working out with weights, Music, and playing word games, chess, reading, and writing.

Enjoy doing Research on Various subjects. (Special interest).
Have Read: 343 Books

Marguerita Rentas   Pedro E. Rentas (RIP)
Josephine Rivera   Jesus Rivera (chuito)

Janixa Lamanica
Auari Lamanica JR.
Aileen Lamanica
Christain Lamanica
Gabriel Lamanica

Joson Rivera
Jason Rivera JR.
Jayden Rivera
Baylee Rivera
Joey Rivera-Muñiz

Carmen Roman
Axle Roman
Johanna Roman
Izaiha TORRES
Angie De-Jesus

Jeremy Roman
Natalia Isabelle-
Roman.

J L TORRES   Linda Marie TORRES
THERE IS NO LUCK IN SUCCESS!

CPSIA information can be obtained
at www.ICGtesting.com
Printed in the USA
BVHW042312100223
658265BV00042B/334/J